Tending Life's Garden

Between Ignorance and Enlightenment (VI)

By
Venerable Master Hsing Yun

Translated by
Venerable Miao Hsi and Cherry Lai

©2005 Buddha's Light Publishing

By Venerable Master Hsing Yun
Translated by Venerable Miao Hsi and Cherry Lai
Edited by Edmond Chang and Robin Stevens
Book designed by Dung Trieu
Cover designed by Chun-Er Cheng

Published by Buddha's Light Publishing
3456 S. Glenmark Drive,
Hacienda Heights, CA 91745, U.S.A.
Tel: (626) 923-5144
Fax: (626) 923-5145
E-mail: itc@blia.org
Website: www.blpusa.com

Protected by copyright under the terms of the International Copyright Union; all rights reserved. Except for fair use in book reviews, no part of this book may be reproduced for any reason by any means, including any method of photographic reproduction, without permission of the publisher. Printed in Taiwan.

ISBN: 1-932293-12-4

CONTENTS

Preface	i
Acknowledgments	v
A Brand New Start	*1*
Daily Renewal	*3*
Accepting Reality	*5*
Tests in Life	*7*
Resolving Problems	*9*
Self-Entrapment	*11*
Overcoming Setbacks	*13*
Going Through Death	*15*
Turning Ourselves Around	*17*
Self-Adjustments	*19*
Habitual Tendencies	*21*
Letting Go of One's Status	*23*
To Adapt and Adjust	*25*
Reforming Ourselves	*27*
Ridding Ourselves of Suffering and Sadness	*29*
Knowing the Way	*31*
Regeneration	*33*
Replacements	*35*
Tending Life's Garden	*37*

Life Skills Education	39
Practical Knowledge	41
Conducting Ourselves	43
Body Language	45
Poise	47
Sportsmanship	49
The Importance of Expressions	51
Cryonics	53
Two-Faced People	55
To Walk in Another's Shoes	57
Likes and Dislikes	59
The Art of Refusing	61
Not Going Against Another's Wishes	63
Sandwich Cookie	65
Understanding the Greater Good	67
Good, Yet Useless People	69
Helping Others Succeed	71
To Perform	73
Think, Speak, Listen, Act	75
Setting a Good Example	77
Self-Deprecation	79
I Assumed	81
The Thought Process	83

Life Planning	*85*
Quality of Life	*87*
The Tracks of Life	*89*
To Save and Prepare	*91*
One's Footing in Life	*93*
Marriage	*95*
One's Family	*98*
Aspects of Human Sentiments	*100*
The Treasure of a Great Friendship	*102*
The Value of Good Neighbors	*104*
The Ways of Home Life	*106*
Nurturing Body and Nature	*108*
Self-Nature	*110*
Moral Life	*112*
Maintenance	*114*
Self-Education	*116*
Governing the Mind	*118*
Purifying the Mind	*120*
Losing Weight	*122*
The Meaning of Rest	*124*
Sculpturing Ourselves	*126*
Maxims	*128*
To Rely on Ourselves	*130*

Develop Our Potential	132
Self-Assurance	134
Self-Respect	136
Having Meaningful Interests	138
Having Tastes in Life	140
Interests and Enthusiasm	142
New Branches on an Old Trunk	144
Passing the Baton	146
Getting On and Off Stage	148
One's Standing in Life	150
Places and Positions	152
Teamwork and Division of Labor	154
The Mind Painter	156
The Wonder of Contemplation	158
On Increasing Positive Thoughts	160
Self-Confidence	162
Motivating Ourselves	164
Expectations and Aspirations	166
The Spring of Life	168
Spreading Joy	170
Interpretations	172
The Study of Life	174
The Metaphors of Life	176

Enigmas	*178*
Having Art in Our Lives	*180*
The Painting of Life	*182*
The True Colors of Life	*184*
Human Nature	*186*
A New Spring for the Elderly	*188*
Life's Golden Age	*190*
Life's Second Spring	*192*
Marathon of Life	*194*
The Transmigration of Life	*196*
The End of Life	*199*
The Non-Duality of Living and Dying	*201*
Glossary	*203*

Preface

It is a privilege for me to contribute this preface as a member of the team of translators and editors that worked on the publication of *Tending Life's Garden*, the sixth volume in English of the popular *Between Ignorance and Enlightenment* series by Venerable Master Hsing Yun. In many ways the process of editing or translating the manuscript is not that different from the experience of a fully engaged reading of this book. This is why I hope what I have to share as an editor will be of some relevance to those who are about to embark on the same profound journey of sound optimism, practical guidance and spiritual liberation I experienced in editing this book. I believe *Tending Life's Garden* can enrich and enlighten all those who are willing to open their hearts and minds to its wisdom and faith. In reading it with diligence and care, we are in essence taking the first key step in "tending to the garden" of our own lives. Each chapter reminds us of what we need to "trim" from our day to day habits, and teaches us how best to "fertilize" our spirit and mind. As Venerable Master Hsing Yun puts it in the title chapter,

> A garden of plum blossoms and lush willows will look forlorn if they are surrounded by withered branches and dead leaves. When our morals and character are flawed, we

cannot win the respect of others no matter how great our accomplishments. Therefore, we should never stop tending to our life's garden, trimming and ridding it of its impurities and decaying matter.

My reading of the first five volumes in the *Between Ignorance and Enlightenment* series left a deep and lasting impact, especially in terms of helping me appreciate how the wisdom of the Dharma can be infused in our daily lives; however, even that realization does not compare to what I have gained from working on *Tending Life's Garden*. It was truly one of those rare instances where the line between "work" and personal cultivation was wonderfully blurred. I am sure much of the reason lies in how deeply immersed I was in the content while editing and proofreading chapter after chapter. Yet, it is also true that there is a powerful and coherent logic that runs throughout this volume that made it particularly illuminating and instructive for me. This logic reveals itself almost in an organic manner, not unlike the blossoming of a flower or the sprouting of leaves on a tree.

In keeping to the theme of "tending life's garden," the book opens with a sequence of chapters that emphasize the need to "trim" and discard the undesirable and decaying aspects of our "garden" in order to provide space and conditions for new and more vibrant growth in our lives. Using the Chan metaphor of "going through death," for example, Venerable Master Hsing Yun reminds us that sometimes renewal and rebirth require us first to discard our old self, to let it "go through death" so to speak, so that a better and more noble self can be born. This means that without death there can be no rebirth or new life; it is needed just as dead leaves are needed as compost to foster new growth in nature. The same applies to unwholesome or harmful habits we may have. As long as we are able to repent and rid ourselves of such sources of suffering and pain, we are able not only to save ourselves, but also to assure ourselves of a brighter future. As Venerable Master Hsing Yun affirms, "In the course of our life, within the day or even the hour, we should constantly 'go through death,' to change our bad ways...When people can transform themselves completely, and turn over a new leaf in life after going through death, it is indeed something to celebrate." This promise of turning over a new leaf captures the spirit of optimism and hope that pervades throughout *Tending Life's Garden*.

Yet, Venerable Master Hsing Yun is also quick to remind us that hope and optimism does not come without the necessary diligence and faith in practicing compassion, loving-kindness, joy and equanimity–the Four Immeasurables espoused in Buddhism–on a daily basis. Again, just as a gardener cannot expect to cultivate a vibrant and prolific garden without tending to it with constant love and care, we also cannot expect to live healthy and fulfilling lives without applying wisdom and discipline to our everyday conduct in life. For this reason, *Tending Life's Garden* is full of specific guidance on how we should tend to our moral, spiritual and emotional "gardens." Discussing topics as poignant and diverse as "The Art of Refusing," "Good, Yet Useless People," "Sandwich Cookies" and "I Assumed," Venerable Master Hsing Yun draws from his wealth of spiritual and worldly knowledge to offer astute and practical guidance on how we should face different life situations, as well as how we should interact with others. In one chapter, he advocates society putting a greater emphasis on a "life skills education." Indeed, much of *Tending Life's Garden* is devoted to that very mission. In another chapter, Venerable Master Hsing Yun points to the importance of having and abiding by "maxims" in life. Likewise, the entire volume is so rich in substance and eloquent in expression that one can find a meaningful "maxim" to follow in almost every chapter.

We should not confuse such an emphasis on adopting "maxims" or pursuing a "life skills education" with a rigid and dogmatic approach on how to live. While it is true that Venerable Master Hsing Yun provides us with sound guidelines in *Tending Life's Garden*, it is equally true that he approaches the challenge of living well more as an art than as dogmatic practice. For this reason, *Tending Life's Garden* is also very rich in artistic metaphors that help to capture the subtleties of living creative and dynamic lives full of meaningful interests and pursuits. Chapters such as "Sculpturing Ourselves" and "The Mind Painter" all rely on the metaphors of art to convey the importance of using positive imagination and wholesome artistry to enhance the quality of our life. At the same time, they remind us that an aesthetic perspective is essential for appreciating the many sources of beauty that is all around us. Venerable Master Hsing Yun conveys this uplifting outlook on life eloquently when he writes,

> We all come into this world with the potential for happiness. There is the beauty in nature, such as that of mountains and rivers, for us to enjoy. We can admire trees, flowers and stars in the sky. We have our families and loved ones to give us tender loving care, society to fulfill our every need, and people with whom we can have many meaningful relationships.

In saying this, he reminds us that life itself is a garden filled with infinite sources for hope, beauty and redemption. As long as we tend to it with loving-kindness, diligence and wisdom, we can all enjoy its teeming beauty and abundant harvest. Picking up and reading this life-affirming and spirit-enriching book is the first key step to tending our life's garden. But taking its lessons and applying them to how we live is crucial for assuring lives of infinite possibility and growth.

Tending Life's Garden is ultimately about affirmation and renewal, just as trimming a favorite rose bush is about expecting it to bloom more beautifully. Venerable Master Hsing Yun captures this spirit perfectly when he writes, "When we pour our life into the stream of the universe, the whole world will jump and dance with us. Then, any season, any age can be the spring of life."

Edmond Chang
Editor

Acknowledgments

We received a lot of help from many people and we want to thank them for their efforts in making the publication of this book possible. We especially appreciate Venerable Tzu Jung, the Chief Executive of the Fo Guang Shan International Translation Center (F.G.S.I.T.C.), Venerable Hui Chi, Abbot of Hsi Lai Temple; Venerable Yi Chao for her support and leadership; Venerable Miao Hsi and Cherry Lai for their translation; Edmond Chang and Robin Stevens for their editing; Mu-Tzen Hsu, Kevin Hsyeh, and Pey-Rong Lee for proofreading and preparing the manuscript for publication; and Dung Trieu for her book design and Chun-Er Cheng for her cover design. Our appreciation also goes to everyone who has supported this project from its conception to its completion.

Tending Life's Garden

Between Ignorance and Enlightenment (VI)

A Brand New Start

How wonderful it is to embark on a brand new start in life! For example, after recovering from a serious illness, we have the opportunity to start over again with a new outlook on life. We may feel down and out, but after working hard, we can gain enough confidence to make a fresh beginning.

In the past, we may have been unwelcome among friends and family, but now we can make good connections with everyone. With the support of friends and classmates, we can launch a brand new start. In the past, we may have been critical and unkind, but today our attitudes have changed for the better. We treat others with courtesy and consideration, and they embrace us with renewed friendship. When we have the confidence it takes to turn over a new leaf, there is hope for success in the future.

Some people sustain serious physical injuries in accidents and become confined to wheelchairs. However, they are still able to move ahead and succeed with great confidence and perseverance. Some people seem to be doomed with ill fate. When they are ready to reap a harvest, a hurricane or flood ruins their crops. On starting a new business, an accident destroys their home or store. However, if their faith in life is still intact, they can start anew and within a few years, success can still be achieved.

If we fall down while walking, we can get up and move on. If our car breaks down on the road, we can get it fixed and drive away. If we fail the entrance examination for college, we can take it again next year. If we lose an election, we can run again next time. Natural disasters like floods, fires, tornadoes or earthquakes may destroy our homes and property, but they can never ruin our faith. If we can start over, we will succeed.

A prominent pianist was struck with polio, became paralyzed, and could no longer work the piano pedals. Although he was forced to retire from performing, he was not discouraged and instead started playing the cello. Through perseverance, and with determination and faith in himself, he eventually became a master cellist.

Victor Stein was a master pianist during the early 20th Century in Vienna, Austria. Unfortunately, his right arm was blown off during World War II. Instead of giving up on his destiny, he pleaded with composers to write music to be played with only the left hand. Later, he became well-known for playing pieces such as the "Left-hand Piano Concerto."

Thomas Edison watched his factory burn down in a fire in which he lost all his possessions. Many worried he could not sustain such a major setback. Much to the surprise of others, he addressed his workers the following day, "I am so thankful that the fire did not destroy me, but rather it burned away all the mistakes I made in the past. We will launch a new beginning today!"

Nine out of ten times in life, our wishes go unfulfilled. This is why we have to learn to get up again when we fall down. Some people can never recover from a single setback. Other people, after overcoming each difficulty, strive on stronger than before. How do we survive falling down and then have the motivation to start anew? I have the following suggestions:

1. Face difficulties with a calm and equanimous mind.
2. Turn adversities around with gratitude.
3. Build up strength with great diligence.
4. Understand causes and conditions with wisdom.

On the journey of life, as long as we have the perseverance to start anew, we will never permanently be knocked down by any setback.

Daily Renewal

Everyday we get up in the morning and clean our homes so that our environment is spic and span. We dress neatly so others will have a fresh and positive impression of us each day. We read newspapers and watch television to find out about current events.

However, we should not only seek the "new" from the outside but also create it from inside our hearts. Our thoughts, views, compassion, our spirit to serve, and our willingness to help others should all be renewed daily. And as we continue to renew our inherent spirit, we are able to elevate our lives to new levels.

Like flowers blooming every spring and trees maturing over the seasons, life flies by day after day. So how can we renew ourselves daily? When we get enough sleep and wake up in the morning enlivened with the spirit to complete something wonderful, we begin our daily renewal. In the evening, joining our palms in front of our shrine of the Buddha and repenting any transgressions we may have committed is another form of renewal. Things are always changing, undergoing the endless cycle of renewal, as are society and technology. When we speak about the X and Y generations, can we afford to remain set in our ways and attached to our views? Can we still not see the good in changing and improving?

Of course, what is new is not necessarily good, nor are all old ways bad. New clothes may not fit as well as our old garments. Similarly, new shoes may hurt our feet, but an old pair feels more comfortable. New friends may be more difficult to get along with, while we find communication becomes easier with old ones.

While we may have new ideas, methods and views, old ethics, relationships, and achievements do not need to be erased completely. People feel insecure in today's society because even though new ethics have not yet been established, the old ones are already being replaced. This is not daily renewal but daily ruin.

In seeking the new, we should not remain set in our ways, stubborn in our attachments, or selfishly obstinate. Moreover, we should never take wrong as right. In our daily renewal, we should follow what is right, be kind to others, be brave in trying new things, rid ourselves of selfishness, and be generous with all. Without giving up the present step, how can we take another and progress toward a new destination?

After World War II, the Japanese awakened to their plight. They changed their former image as warmongers and tirelessly developed new industries and products. Today, they have "conquered" America with Toyota cars. We do not wish for powerful countries in the world to conquer their neighbors with weapons and war. We only wish for new ideas, views, trends, products, methods, and ethics to influence the world and enhance peace.

In the past, we revered stores over a hundred years old. However, if these stores fail to infuse new blood, spirit and methods, how long can they last in the end? In Buddhism, the truths of the Three Dharma Seals, Four Noble Truths, and Doctrine of Emptiness do not change. However, when systems, precepts, liturgies, Dharma instruments and functions, constructions, and cultural objects remain unchanged and resistant to renewal, their future development is worrisome.

Many people fear the "new" because new things are not easy to adjust to or understand. While history is a mirror, it should not only reflect the past because we need to see the future. Daily renewal may be just a little flower, but it blooms every day giving us surprising delights. So, why should we fear it?

Accepting Reality

There are things in the world that we can and cannot change. The wind blows, the rain pours down, and we inevitably grow old over the years, regardless of what we do to avoid it. There are things in life that cannot be overcome, like the suffering one might endure from a terminal disease; the experiences of birth, aging, sickness, and death in life; the existence, abidance, decay, and extinction of the world; the arising, existence, change, and cessation of the mind; and the retributions of cause and effect.

In order to change the things that we can, we need wisdom, willpower, and human connections. Poverty can be overcome with hard work, and difficulties and setbacks can be resolved with strength and perseverance. Gossip and chaos can be eradicated if we are wise; obstacles can be overcome when we have assistance and the right connections.

People who cannot accept reality often suspect others are laughing at them upon hearing even a single negative word uttered unintentionally. They retreat and hide, losing the courage to connect with others. In order to conceal their shortcomings, they tend to act defensively. Like porcupines, they are difficult to approach. In the end, they are only harming themselves and hurting those who care for them.

When faced with realities that cannot be changed, we must accept them before we can find new paths. For instance, in accepting the devastation of wind and rain, we can fortify ourselves to respond to future storms more effectively. In facing the harsh reality of setbacks, we can start over again with new resolve. Accepting the vicissitudes of human relations allows us to learn to adjust to circumstances as they arise. We can turn a new leaf in life after we accept the devastation of loss; we can better overcome anxiety when we face danger and fear.

Across the ages, people who could accept poverty, suffering, and physical handicaps were often inspired with great courage and spirit to improve themselves and make adjustments in their lives. They succeeded in creating beautiful lives for themselves. For example, Helen Keller overcame the drawbacks of blindness and became an inspiration for others with her work. Thomas Edison continued his research after his laboratory burned down. Beethoven lost his hearing and wrote Symphony No. 9. Franklin Roosevelt was stricken with polio and still won a fourth term as president. These people all faced realities that could not be changed. However, they changed their lives with will-power and perseverance.

There is a saying, "Try your best and obey the will of heaven." Accepting reality is not being pessimistic but is starting over again with positive resolve. It is not giving up hope; it is being endlessly hopeful. It is not wallowing in defeat but embarking on a new road to success. It is not retreating but facing ourselves more honestly. It is not falling down for good but reorganizing for another advance. By accepting reality and being optimistic and progressive, we make up for our shortcomings.

Tests in Life

There are many tests in life. At home, our parents test us to see if we are respectful, useful, and able to do well later in life. As we enter school, our teachers test and observe us to see if we are intelligent, studious, and courteous.

Growing up, we make friends and fall in love. Our friends and lovers test our loyalty, sense of responsibility, character, maturity and stability, all in order to determine if they should spend their lives with us. On entering the workforce, our academic qualifications and work experience are similarly assessed. We go through interviews and even written tests in applying for a position and can only be accepted when every aspect of our character, abilities, and special talents meet all the requirements.

Our presence in society is also constantly under watchful eyes that scrutinize us for the extent of our academic learning, reasoning, and morals to decide whether we are good enough to befriend. When young men and women enlist to serve in the armed forces, they are assessed on the basis of their family backgrounds and on whether they have a criminal record. At home, the members of our family may not say it openly, but they observe if our finances are healthy, the friends we make are good, and whether our behavior is ethical. They, too, scrutinize us.

As we enter middle and old age, we often get physical examinations in hospitals and clinics to check our blood pressure, blood sugar level, cholesterol, etc. We are x-rayed, scanned, and tested for the exact state of our health. However, even after going through the many tests and exams, we still may not be sure if our health meets the standards.

Traveling to other countries, we have to answer questions posed by immigration officers, and at home, the census office conducts surveys on a regular basis. In obtaining any special qualifications, we must pass different kinds of tests. For instance, we are tested in order to get our driver's and contractor's licenses. Even our performance on musical instruments or in sports like Tae Kwon Do is assessed.

From kindergarten to elementary and secondary schools, and college to graduate schools, we have to pass all kinds of tests in order to enter and graduate from each institution. Similarly, we have to make the grade at different stages in life. However, if we fail one test after another, life will surely be more difficult.

Therefore, as long as we are still breathing, we need to learn to improve ourselves so that we have what it takes to pass the different tests life has in store for us.

Resolving Problems

There are many problems in life that need to be resolved. The capable will think of ways to deal with them, while others will look for excuses to pass the buck.

After birth, the first test we face is our health. If we do not have the immunity to fight diseases, we can easily die. Therefore, getting vaccinated resolves our first problem. As we grow up and go to school, we face numerous tests from elementary school all the way to college and even graduate school if we pursue advanced study. We will be tested on our understanding of what we learn. Upon leaving school, we have to pass written exams and interview for jobs, a test of our ability to resolve problems at work.

In society, besides dealing with the problem of making a living, we have to face situations related to human relations, finance, marriage, and career. We worry about our country and community, and concern ourselves with our parents and children. Life is truly complicated.

Nowadays, when faced with problems at work or in their studies, some people become lost and choose to kill themselves. This is a cowardly attempt to evade reality and is no way to solve problems. When problems surface, we need to first tell ourselves, "Be brave in facing them, and don't retreat." For instance, when we fail an exam, we need to know whether it is due to our lack of preparation or if it is because we are taking the wrong direction in our studies. After we find out, we have to pursue the right path and work hard. If we are rejected after applying for a job, we have to find out whether there were candidates with better qualifications or if we were too nervous in the interview. On discovering the reason, we should face reality with calm minds and work to improve ourselves further. If a relationship with a loved one ends, we should reflect on whether it was because of personality clashes or differences in education and family backgrounds. By digging up the truth, we can try to salvage the relationship. Otherwise, we can look for another person who is more compatible, or simply decide, "I existed quite happily by myself before, so it is probably possible again."

After determining what the problem is, we should make adjustments accordingly. We need to take a step back and be considerate of others. By being able to work with our disadvantages and by being humble, we can gain the approval of the people around us and eventually become a winner.

The biggest difficulty in resolving problems is not knowing where the problem lies. When we do not even know what the problem is, how are we going to solve it? However, as the saying goes, "Those involved are often lost while onlookers can see clearly." If we cannot discover the problem, we can ask someone else to help. When others take the initiative to tell us, we should be humble and accept their advice. However, if we keep passing the buck, there will be no way to solve it. Resolving problems is the motivation behind overcoming difficulties and making progress. It is like removing a rock on the road blocking our way. When we do not have the strength to do it on our own, we should seek the help of benevolent friends or listen to the experience of our elders. However, if we keep avoiding the problem, the path will forever be blocked by the rock and we will not be able to move forward in life.

Self-Entrapment

A silkworm spins a cocoon to wrap around itself before it transforms into a moth. But when people do the same, they are spinning a trap that entangles them. If we cannot transcend the troubles caused by greed and anger, fail to distance ourselves from arrogance, conceit, and delusion, and have problems with drugs, alcoholism, and gambling, we are causing our own entrapment. We are simply giving up our freedom. There have been a number of movie stars in the last few decades who killed themselves for love. They did so because they failed to turn themselves around or to create a buffer for themselves in their love life. They chose to walk on the path of no return.

So many people around us are attached to their views and cannot accept the suggestions of others. Some are deeply entrenched in the gully of greed and fail to be content or grateful for what they have. They hold on to their old and inadequate ways, refusing to accept new knowledge. Because they are too stubborn and have an unclear understanding of the situation, they close themselves off and are unwilling to take any steps to free themselves from the entrapment of their own cocoons. When people do not have the right view and are taken in by cults or fail to unite allowing their organizations to split up, they are also creating their own entrapments.

Throughout Chinese history numerous examples abound in which people snared themselves in traps of their own making, thus bringing about their demise. During the Epoch of the Warring States, Shang Yang established very strict laws and severe penalties, but he ended up dying by his own laws. During the early days of the republic, Yuan Shikai was overcome by his greed for power and status in his attempt to become the emperor. Subsequently, he was forced to announce the end of his short reign when his scheme failed. He eventually got sick and died from frustration.

As the popular saying goes, "The one untying the bell has to be the one who tied it in the first place." When we trap ourselves in a cocoon, we are the only ones able to break out of it. Song Dynasty poet Lu You asserted, "Life is like spring silkworms spinning a cocoon to bind themselves. Once the body is fully grown, we have to break through by ourselves." Therefore, even when others are willing to tear open the cocoon for us, we still need to have the will to come out on our own!

German writer Goethe wrote the novel *Wilhelm Meister's Apprenticeship*, describing himself at twenty-five years of age and how he endured the pain of falling out of love and his good friend's suicide because of lost love. After reading the book, many young people, surprisingly, took their own lives. When we drive ourselves to a dead end with self-imposed restrictions, we leave ourselves no way out. We are simply spinning our own cocoons without having the courage to break out of them.

In order to break out of our cocoons, we must accept the tests of setbacks and pain and subdue our cravings and attachments. We need to learn to self-reflect and accept failure. We must be able to enhance our knowledge with new things and make the right friends to broaden our vistas.

We are tested in various ways at different stages of life. If we can withstand the attacks of wind and rain and can still break out of the cocoon to stand firmly on our ground, and if we are able to survive the tempering of setbacks to mature and grow strong, then we will tread on the path of success.

Overcoming Setbacks

In order to be successful in our personal lives and careers, we need the help of many positive causes and conditions, in the same way trees and plants need sunshine, fresh air, and water to flourish, or buildings require materials such as timber, cement, steel, and masonry to be constructed. When causes and conditions are right for us, it is easy to accomplish what we set out to do. When they are not going our way, we face obstacles and difficulties at every turn in life.

Although setbacks and difficulties may defeat an ordinary person, they cannot overcome a capable young person. This is because unfavorable causes and conditions can motivate a person to develop his/her potential. They are adverse forces that can actually spur progress. For example, when we are ill, we know we should pursue a path of cultivation and care more about our health. When we suffer, we realize we should improve our situation by working hard.

In the world of nature, plum blossoms are often praised because they can withstand ice and snow, and become more fragrant as a result. Pines and cypresses are admired because they can endure the frost and cold, and grow greener as it gets colder. A bamboo tree stands straight and tall in the high winds and rains, while many animals strive bravely to survive the icy tundra of the North and South Poles.

Wherever we look, we see many other examples of those who overcome obstacles. When trees are uprooted by storms, we can straighten and replant them. When houses are toppled by an earthquake, we can rebuild them. A young person who suffers the discrimination and intimidation of others will work harder and strive against all odds to succeed. Just as a ball bounces higher when hit harder, we witness many physically challenged people overcome disabilities and become successful athletes, painters, and writers. Children from poor families often grow up to be high achievers. In practicing Chan Buddhism, practitioners are often encouraged to travel to cold places in the winter and hot places in the summer to experience life under adverse circumstances.

Had it not been for its persecution under the rule of some imperial dynasties, Chinese Buddhism would not have realized its full strength and glory. For example, without the authoritarian rule and oppression of the emperor, Venerable Master Huiyuan would not have been motivated to declare "Monastics do not have to pay homage to the monarchy." Without the betrayal of Judas, the holiness of Jesus would not have been made more apparent. Without the persecutions of his disciples Devadatta and Angulimalya, the Buddha's high morals and magnanimity would not have been evident. Therefore, we should not fear setbacks. When we encounter stumbling blocks on the path of life, we may either trip over them, or we may use them as stepping stones on which we can climb to see far and wide.

Our success in life depends on whether or not we can overcome setbacks and turn them into conditions for progress. When there is no darkness, there is no brightness, and without vices and mistakes we cannot discover the good and the beautiful. When there is no filth, we cannot appreciate cleanliness, and without differences there will be no unity.

Going Through Death

In Chan Buddhism, there is a form of teaching that describes how a person progresses from ignorance to enlightenment, a process which is referred to as "going through death." It illustrates how in the transmigration of life, except for our true mind, our habitual tendencies, worries, and ignorance must all experience many cycles of life and death before we are finally liberated. If we evaluate just this current life, we can see how many unwholesome habits we have, how selfish we can be, and the endless attachments we carry. Without "going through death" and releasing the burden of these things, we cannot be reborn.

Buddhism identifies two patterns in explaining living and dying. The first takes place in stages, and the other through changes. Therefore, besides the lives and deaths that we experience as we transmigrate within the six planes of existence, we need to radically transform our characteristics and habitual tendencies before we can be liberated.

Chinese poet Tao Yuanming wrote, "By realizing what I did not understand clearly in the past, I know I can still pursue and change in the future." A person needs to "go though death" before awakening to the concept that "What happened in the past died yesterday, and what will happen in the future is born today." Life after going through death is like a snake shedding its skin, a cicada its case, and a lobster its shell. By going through the process, a person can attain further achievements.

King Asoka of ancient India was a violent, warmongering invader. Most people called him "Black Asoka." However, after he embraced the Dharma and practiced benevolence to improve the welfare of his people, he gained a good reputation for both himself and the country. He earned the name "White Asoka" as a result.

If he had not "gone through death," how could the king have transformed himself from Black Asoka to White Asoka? If a person does not "put down the butcher knife," how can he/she "become a Buddha here and now?" In the Jataka stories of the Buddha's previous lives, the

Buddha cut his flesh to feed an eagle and gave himself up to feed a tigress. His deeds and spirit of sacrificing himself to help other sentient beings illustrate that it takes "going through death" before one can attain Buddhahood.

There was once a scoundrel in Japan whom people called "the demon-warrior." He bullied good people and took advantage of his neighbors. Even his only young son was not spared from his abuse and viciousness. One day, he was very hungry and overheard someone ask his son, "Why don't you eat the food you have?"

His son replied, "I'm saving it for my father!" What the boy said touched his father's true heart so much that the man was moved to tears. From then on, he repented his violence and malice. After going through the death of his past, he became helpful toward his neighbors, and loving and protective of his family. So people no longer called him "the demon-warrior" but "the Buddha" instead.

It does not matter how many unwholesome habits we have or mistakes we have made. As long as we are willing to repent and "go through death," we can save ourselves. For instance, if swearing at people is one of our bad habits, by being aware of our speech, we can change the way we speak. If we take control of our unwholesome acts, we can transform our behavior. Therefore, in the course of life, we should "go through death" continuously, every day and every hour, in order to reform our bad ways. Then, we will not need to worry about our ability to succeed.

Some people need to experience "going through death" themselves in order to improve and progress through extreme pain and suffering. Other people see others' suffering and are able to feel and learn by example.

When ex-convicts leave prison, they need to "go through death." Otherwise, if their vicious nature is not changed, their devious habits will recur. When people transform themselves completely and turn over a new leaf in life after going through death, it is indeed something to celebrate.

Turning Ourselves Around

"Turn around and the shore is there." This well-known saying is a good reminder in life. When the prodigal turns around and changes for the better, he/she is as good as gold. If an individual fails to see what is ahead and charges forward blindly, the result will be either crashing into a wall or falling over the cliff. Therefore, knowing when to turn around is very important.

The journey of life is full of temptation and traps. When lured by temptation, if we do not turn ourselves around in time, we may find ourselves on the road of no return. For instance, many people indulge themselves in sex and alcohol. They should know when to turn things around, because their fate is in their own hands. Others blindly pursue fame and high status, not realizing how their lives have become shackled by their pursuits. If they turn their minds around, they will be so much more carefree.

By looking ahead, we can only see half of the world. But by turning around, we will find the other half. The world in front is like a narrow door everyone is fighting to go through, and someone is bound to get hurt. If we can turn around and look at the world behind us, where there is no one fighting, we will see it is so much more open and free!

In life's boundless ocean of suffering, it is important for us to turn around to look for the shore. When we are forced into a corner by circumstances, or find ourselves walking down a dead-end alley because of our thoughts, it is crucial that we know how to turn things around and give ourselves some space. Just as in driving a car, we should know how to make a turn ahead of time. When crossing each other's path on the street, we need to know when to step aside. We should ask ourselves, "Is it really victory for us when we do not yield and move?"

There are so many embarrassing situations where we need to find a way out. Similarly, when we are engaged in conflicts with others, we should step back to look for a solution. Without leaving enough ground for negotiation in our relationships with others, we will not be able to reap good results. When there are financial disputes, we need to leave enough space for both sides to turn the situation around. Whatever the situation, when we are faced with obstacles, we have to understand when and how to turn ourselves around.

As the saying goes, "Reaching the end of mountains or rivers, we naturally need to turn around." Sailing in an ocean of suffering, we must understand that because the ocean is boundless, we must turn around to find the shore. In moving down the path of life, we also need to know where to turn around.

There is a verse on the front gates of Fo Guang Shan in Taiwan, "Where do you want to go? Please consider carefully when you plan to come back! Turn around and the shore is there." Once we understand this concept, need we still fear not having room to turn ourselves around in life?

Self-Adjustments

On the journey of life, we may run into dead ends or face insurmountable obstacles. In such cases, we need to know how to turn ourselves around. When we change our direction and views, we will most likely find another path. For example, we may find that our food is too salty, bland, sour, or spicy. But if we season it appropriately, the flavor can be adjusted to our tastes. There are innumerable situations in which we need to make adjustments.

A couple may argue from time to time. They should use respect and tolerance to make adjustments in their relationship. Friends may hold different views or have misunderstandings. They should be open and sincere in their exchange of opinions in order to amend their differences.

There are many people who work in high paying jobs or lucrative businesses. However, they should not be spendthrifts, and should instead learn to exercise control over their spending. When they enjoy good days, they should remember times when there were shortages. On the other hand, people who lose their jobs during economic slowdowns should be willing to let go of their past glory and earn a living with lower pay and harder work. They should adjust themselves and be willing to live a simple life of lesser means. This way, they can live their days in ease and joy.

In dealing with lost love, we should appreciate and accept that the conditions were not right. We should remember that "As there are many stars in the sky, there are many more people on earth. Why suffer because of one person?" If we fail an exam, we should bear in mind that we may not have prepared well enough, and that it is all right for us to try again next time and work harder.

When others reject us for being arrogant, we should change and be humble. If anger is our shortcoming, we need to adjust and learn to treat others with compassion. If others find us stingy, we should be more generous and make broad connections with them. If being too aloof and eccentric is our problem, we need to learn to be more accommodating when circumstances demand it, so that we can get along with others.

As long as we know how to adjust and turn a situation around, there is nothing we cannot change. When the temperatures drop, we put on warmer clothes to adjust to weather changes. When we are hungry or thirsty, we eat or drink to meet our physical needs. People who are able to self-adjust can reach a new plane in handling daily living, their emotions, finances, or the ways of the world.

Some people cannot adjust well at times. When they face a little difficulty, they feel there are roadblocks everywhere they go. Bound by their plight, they plummet into depression. They sit and worry, failing to liberate themselves from its confines. Not being flexible is indeed ignorant and one of the greatest weaknesses in life.

Governments today need to adjust all the time. When faced with stalemates in diplomacy, they change their foreign policy. In dealing with economic recessions, they have experts to help make strategic changes that stimulate consumption and adjust supply and demand in order to jumpstart the economy. Lawmakers are always amending various propositions and measures to meet the needs and demands of the general public so that laws can be passed. Similarly, constant reforms are required in education in order to keep up with changing times.

Living in a complicated, constantly changing world, we need to apply much effort. We must be equipped well to deal with the different levels of knowledge, morals, abilities, moods, and human relationships that exist. However, being able to self-adjust is most important. Friends, how do you adjust to your environment, careers, friendships, and much more?

Habitual Tendencies

Habitual tendencies are habits we have acquired over time. There are many kinds of habitual tendencies. There are positive ones like enjoying reading, listening to music, making donations, and practicing benevolence, and less wholesome ones, such as napping during the day, procrastinating, impulsive shopping, and tardiness.

Newton's Law of Inertia states that if a body is at rest or moving at a constant speed in a straight line, it will continue to do so unless it is acted upon by a force. People's wholesome and unwholesome habitual tendencies are similar. If we do not self-reflect and improve, the small habits and actions we make will become habitual tendencies over time.

A habitual tendency can be imperceptible, like the earth revolving around the sun every day without anyone noticing. We habitually do things without even realizing how they affect others; for instance, we frown at people, take things without asking, talk loudly, use foul language, jerk our heads and bodies while walking or sitting, make indiscreet facial expressions, tell lies, and act meanly toward others. We may tend to be lazy, fool around, seek unwarranted connections with the rich and famous, gossip, use flattery, and smoke and drink too much, all without realizing it. As the saying goes, "It is like walking into a fish market so often that you no longer smell its odor."

On the other hand, there are good habitual tendencies, such as working without complaints despite hardship and criticism, picking up after others, taking joy in another's good deeds, speaking kind words, being diligent at work and study, saving money, and happily helping people. Other examples are having a good sense of humor, sharing a laugh with others, being optimistic, and exercising regularly.

The *Bhiksuni Mahaprajapati Sutra* mentions the "eighty-four manners of women," which are actually women's eighty-four habitual tendencies. In the *Vibhasa Sastra*, it is said that Pilindavatsa, a disciple of the Buddha, had been a Brahman for five hundred lives in the past and was very arrogant. He was used to calling on his maids to serve him and every time he crossed the Ganges River, he addressed the river god as "Little Maid." Even though the Buddha told him to repent, out of habit he said, "Little Maid, don't be angry. I apologize to you and repent my transgression." And though the head disciple of the Buddha, Mahakasyapa, was foremost in practicing asceticism, once, upon hearing four music gods playing instruments, he instinctively started to dance. It turns out that in one of his previous lives, he had been a dancer. After we have acquired habitual tendencies, it is very hard to change them.

Bai Juyi, a famed poet of the Tang Dynasty, once wrote, "When one is used to listening to songs and music, one will not know about spears and arrows." Mencius said, "We survive in hardships and difficulties but die in ease and peace." These examples point out that if people are too accustomed to a life of ease, it can create a crisis for a country. In addition to personal habitual tendencies, our living environment and corporations can also take on habits. While habitual tendencies are not necessarily bad, even good ones need to be adjusted appropriately over time. Otherwise, we will not be in step with society and can be easily left behind.

When we change our unwholesome, personal habits, we can improve. When corporations do so, they can open up new opportunities, and when national defense adjusts its protocols, the country will be more alert to possible crisis. When we change our habits, life will be much more interesting. The *History of the Later Han* observed, "Without polishing and reforming oneself, one will sink into lowly habits." Therefore, if we have unwholesome habits, we must have the resolve to correct them so that they will not develop into harmful ones.

Letting Go of One's Status

"Status" or "position" is a relative concept conceived in the eyes of the beholder. While some people consider their family background a status symbol, others use their education or wealth as leverage to be different or superior. Those who are either talented or famous might feel more dignified because of their prestige. However, it is indeed very inappropriate for society to rely on fame, fortune, or power as the means by which we measure social worth.

If a family name alone can give a person social status, then the descendants of Confucius and other virtuous men and women would automatically have the respect of their contemporaries. However, respect is something that must be earned. It must be won through hard work and the willingness not only to carry on, but also to live up to one's family name and tradition. Although there are people who have put their faith in the power of money to elevate their social positions, having money does not necessarily accrue the merits of generosity. A miser can never have the respect of society despite the fact that he/she may be very rich. Without humility and sincerity, a person of talent or education is limited in life.

Throughout history, it has not been uncommon for famous people to avoid the limelight for a simple life in the pursuit of true happiness. It was not unusual for kings and rulers to suffer indignity for the sake of survival and the hope of returning to power one day. The last emperor of China was perfectly content in his role as a commoner and a gardener for the Beijing Park when the Communist Party rose to power.

When a wise ruler wanted to gain a better understanding of the needs of his people, he would travel the land in disguise and live among them as an ordinary person. He shared not only their joys but also their sorrows as if they were his own. When a CEO of a large corporation wished to know the feelings of his employees, he tried to walk in their shoes and share their experiences. Taipei Mayor Ma Yingjiou has become one of the most popular figures in Taiwan because of his down-to-earth style. On any given day, when he is not busy with his mayoral duties, he takes off his coat and tie to jog in the park with people or play a game of basketball on a public court.

In today's society, many people are unwilling to take a job that they think is below their status, for it makes them feel ashamed and humiliated. They have, however, ignored the fact that the world's economy is in a recession now, and economic growth has hit all-time lows. Companies are forced to lay off their workers, and an increasing number of people have joined the ranks of the unemployed. If a person cannot leave past glories behind and lower his expectations, he will have difficulty finding anything, not to speak of a job that is befitting of his former status. However, if he realizes that a job is hard to come by in today's market and accepts any work that is available, he will not only survive the present, but will also have another chance for a better future.

The inability or the unwillingness for us to let go of our status and be humble is an attachment. Since our purpose in life is to find happiness, we must learn to let go of all attachments in the course of our pursuits and be as carefree as possible. If we want to be truly happy, we must not be angry or annoyed when someone says or does something wrong. If we want to rid ourselves of worries and defilement, we must learn to loosen our grip and be indifferent toward that which is not worthy of our attention, such as fame, power, fortune, gossip, pleasure, and desires. Only through the practice of non-grasping will we be able to live happily in the moment according to our situation.

To Adapt and Adjust

From the moment we are born, we gradually learn to adapt to our surroundings. We wave our arms and legs to win the laughter of our parents, and cry and smile to attract the attention of those around us. When we reach adulthood and enter society, we learn to adapt ourselves in a totally different way. While some people rely on the rules of morality to guide them through the many changes of life, others turn to crime and violence as their chosen recourse.

"Survival of the fittest" is actually a test to determine our ability to adapt and adjust to crises in our daily environment, aside from responding to natural catastrophes, such as earthquakes, floods, or droughts. Sometimes, the ability to adapt and adjust is merely a biological reaction to matters that nobody has any control over, like a change in weather or temperature. Just as a compressor needs to constantly adjust itself to different currents of electricity, people need to adapt and adjust themselves to different situations for the sake of self-preservation.

Global politics is so unpredictable and tumultuous today that it is truly a challenge for any diplomat to adapt to changing conditions. Similarly, a driver must be very cautious in adjusting to the flow of traffic if he/she is to be safe and accident-free. Some animals are able to camouflage themselves by adjusting to the colors of their natural environment. The human heart, however, is harder to gauge, because it more often than not adjusts according to the dictates of self-interest.

In Britain, women have long worn hats in public, but some refuse to take them off even in theaters, thus obstructing the view of others in the audience. In an effort to remedy this awkward situation, the government made the following announcement: "We welcome all *elderly* ladies of the country to wear their high-hats at all times!" Since then, women have become more conscious and considerate of their choice of headgear on account of the government's ability in this case to respond with humor.

New York City was devastated by the 9/11 terrorist attack, but it was able to recover quickly without too many obstacles because of Mayor Rudy Giuliani's rapid response to the tragedy. Later that year, the mayor was named *Time Magazine's* "Person of the Year" for his efforts to bring a sense of normalcy back to the people of New York.

The Buddha taught in accordance with his disciples' mental dispositions. He would expound different teachings to different people with regard to their abilities and levels of understanding. He would teach the truth of emptiness or the phenomenon of existence, the Law of Dependent Origination or the difference between conventional and ultimate truth. He constantly adapted and adjusted his teachings as the occasion and audience dictated. Therefore, we can say that the Dharma as discoursed by the Buddha is the result of adaptive teaching.

Although we must constantly adapt and adjust ourselves, we must never lose sight of our principles. We must bear in mind that no matter how the Dharma has adapted itself to the changes of impermanence, it has never contradicted the truth. Thus, we should remain principled in our responses and responsive in our principles. We should never abandon them, either by following conditions indiscriminately or by stubbornly refusing to accept conditions because of them. This is the best way for us to adapt and adjust to an impermanent world.

Reforming Ourselves

We make alterations to our clothes when they no longer fit well or to products if they are not up to standard. When a country or an organization is not in step with the times, it needs to be reformed. And if our views are incorrect, we must change them, or we may not be able to survive.

Young women concerned about looking pretty will not hesitate to make over features such as their eyes, nose, and complexion. They are eager to enhance their looks in order to appear more attractive. People with resolve want to transform their laziness and apathy into active progress. Those who are slow and miserly wish to become generous and wise; the narrow-minded and individualistic wish to be tolerant and compassionate; and the selfish and arrogant wish to become humble and selfless.

Professionals in different fields are also always active in making improvements. Scientists research genetic engineering; agriculturalists work to improve different plant species; politicians change their policies; educators reform the ways they teach; and public figures attempt to transform their image. Everyone seeks change and progress on their path to success.

Some people chase after a good life, wealth, a high position, security, good health, dreams, or goals. They go to fortune-tellers or pray to deities with the hope of getting help. In reality, they are much better off transforming themselves instead. They are always looking for the support of those with power and influence to provide the pull needed to rise to a higher level, but these efforts are not as realistic and beneficial as self-reform.

The ancients said, "While it is hard to reach heaven, asking another for help is more difficult." Therefore, instead of wishing for good fate, luck, and accidental fortune, we should try to transform our own causes and conditions to get better results. Throughout history, despots such as Nero, Hitler, and Mussolini persisted in their own delusions with no intention of self-reform. In the end, all they did was leave behind infamous reputations in the annals of history.

The greatest shortcoming in life is the refusal to reform ourselves, which means we are reluctant to face ourselves and unwilling to progress. Who is, after all, born a great hero or a saint? Only endless reform will help us move closer to perfection.

King Asoka of ancient India had a cruel and vicious nature, so people called him the "Black Asoka." After he reformed himself and became a devout Buddhist practitioner, he engaged in charity work, built hospitals, compiled Buddhist scriptures, and eventually became known as the "White Asoka." If the Buddha's son, Rahula, had not changed his unwholesome habit of telling lies, how could he have become one of the Buddha's ten greatest disciples?

We all have faults as none of us are saints, but if we are willing to change them, there is no greater virtue. Our worst shortcoming is always looking for excuses and not knowing how to change ourselves. If we can reform our shortcomings, such as selfishness, attachment to our views, envy, laziness, greed, and anger, we can accomplish anything we want.

Ridding Ourselves of Suffering and Sadness

A Chinese poet once wrote, "How much suffering can one bear? It is as much as a river flowing to the East in spring." The sadness and frustrations in life can be really harmful to our well-being. When we look at society, it seems that everyone is trapped in unhappiness at some point or another. When one's mind is depressed, it is like being possessed by evil spirits from which there is no release.

Some people are saddened by war and death or with the memory of loved ones gone. Others are depressed because of broken families, the loss of a job, or failure in school. All in all, when there is no hope or satisfaction in life, and when we feel short-changed or even bullied and cannot share the pain with anyone, we end up suffering in many ways.

We can easily see how many people suffer because of their never-ending troubles. Some cannot sleep at night because of gossip by others. A simple matter may bring endless misery and discomfort. A few unintentional, hurtful, or inconsiderate words may trigger loss of appetite and moodiness. Precious time in life is thus lost amidst sadness and frustration. This is truly regrettable!

Another Chinese poet wrote, "Even the largest boat cannot carry all the woes in the world." It is an illustration of the prevalence and weight of life's misery. But in reality, many people are simply getting upset over nothing. Most of the time, they are causing their own sadness or frustrations. Chan Buddhism teaches, "There is nothing to bind you; it is you binding yourself!" Nobody is imposing suffering on us. Most often, we are just bringing it on ourselves!

We can learn to use wisdom and reasoning to ease sorrow and unhappiness. The best way to do so is through faith. The following are some of the ways to reduce unhappiness:
1. Be optimistic and hopeful.
2. Apply reason in dealing with all people, things, situations, and matters.

3. Learn to control your mood.
4. Do not be suspicious; instead, trust others.
5. Actively serve and help others.
6. Face life openly and honestly.

"How much suffering can one bear? It is as much as a river flowing to the East in spring." However, as long as we can be open-minded and let go of our attachments, sadness in life can easily become the source of our enlightenment.

Knowing the Way

There is a Chinese saying, "Wealth and prosperity access the four seas; fortune and glory reach the three rivers." When there is access to fame and fortune, we can spread out in all ten directions. However, we need to know the right way to accomplish this in order to develop good human relationships, careers, and correct speech.

When we travel, we must know the path and directions before we can reach our destination. In work, we should have knowledge of certain skills and methods in order to get the job done. If we do not know the way and fall on the wrong track or get lost in the process, it will be very difficult to reach our goals.

The roadways in the world are not only limited to geographical ones. Everywhere we go there are passages in money, politics, human relations, knowledge, and society. If we want to make money, we need capital, diligence, good connections, expedient means, concern for others' well-being, and the ability to overcome difficulties. All are ways to make a profit. Our bank accounts, employees, and solutions are also paths to making money. Without them, we will not have a chance at making a fortune.

In our studies, good teachers, right thinking, assimilation of knowledge, reasoning, and practice are all necessary for success. Our career or business requires good human connections, functional products, good use of personnel, and praise of others. In human relations, we also need to know our way. For instance, kind words, benevolent deeds, generosity, service, integrity, and trustworthiness are all paths leading to harmony with others. In love, friendship, family, home life, or assistance from others, there are also appropriate ways to ensure smooth relationships.

People nowadays often neglect passageways. After they build a house, they start bickering with the neighbors about right of way. They may buy a lot of land but forget to leave roadways for themselves. In addition they often ruin their own paths with unwholesome hobbies, decadence, wastefulness, laziness, aggressive behavior, grudges, making enemies, greed, and extortion.

If roadways between countries are blocked, how can society progress? When the connections between people are obstructed, how do we deal with situations? If the divide between self and others is deep and there are walls and mountains blocking the paths in human relations, how do we develop?

There are different ways to communicate well with our superiors and keep in touch with our subordinates at work. It was because every road led to the Tang Dynasty capital, Changan, that it prospered. If we have a good network of pathways in dealing with people and our affairs, we need not fear failure.

Regeneration

Great strides have been made in society, not only in the arts, sciences, and quality of life, but also in our relationships to nature and daily necessities. Of all the advancements in our lives, the concept of "regeneration" is most valuable. For example, we now have recycled products, redeveloped land, reclamation projects, and filtrated recycled water. Even people "regenerate" themselves in many different ways. Couples renew their love after a short time out following petty squabbles. Life-and-death friends reunite to share stories of grief and sorrow. Criminals repent their mistakes to start a new life. Juveniles who had gone astray and disappointed their parents mend their ways and turn over a new leaf when given a second chance. In addition to these examples of "regeneration" in human conduct, human organs can also be healed and regenerated through surgery and proper medication.

Anything that can be recycled or regenerated, such as a human life or a human organ, is very valuable because regeneration makes things stronger and life more precious. Hiroshima overcame its fate as the first city demolished by an atomic bomb to become one of the most beautiful and modern cities in the world. Tang Shan, China, rose from the rubble of a deadly earthquake to become a new city. When Taiwan was devastated by a powerful earthquake in 1999, its citizens courageously came together to rebuild their lives and make their homeland stronger and more beautiful. Therefore, as long as we are confident in ourselves and have the right conditions, regeneration is always possible. Farmers and engineers have successfully reprocessed used fertilizers. Survivors of catastrophes have regained their strength. Just as lost teeth and hair can grow again, trash and land can be recycled and reclaimed. Today, we have already genetically reproduced cows, sheep, and pigs, and perhaps we will even do so with humans in the near future.

"Spring will come to the withered tree, and a dying flower will live to see another day." Although death is inevitable, there is always rebirth after death. With the coming of winter, spring is just around the corner. As long as there is rebirth, there will be hope; as long as there is hope, there will be life after death. A capable physician can work miracles to bring a dying patient back to life. A skillful sculptor can give life to the lifeless, because he possesses the ability to work wonders with any material. Thus, regeneration is a very valuable process.

Nowadays, people are often interested in the question of living and dying. No matter how mysterious the subject seems to be, it is in fact very simple. Death and rebirth is an endless cycle. Although some people have made many mistakes at a young age, they must not feel ashamed because a new lease on life is possible when they have the courage to face their mistakes and are determined in their efforts to start anew. Is it not true that a criminal who has paid his debts to society can make a significant contribution if he is willing to use his mind and skills for the good of the people?

Throughout history, we have seen examples of how a country can restore its prestige and glory after unbearable hardships. After Japan was forced to surrender unconditionally at the end of World War II, it worked relentlessly to rebuild itself as one of the world's superpowers fifty years later. Therefore, failure is the mother of all success, and we should not be deterred by temporary setbacks. As long as we have confidence in ourselves to renew our lives, we need not worry about our future.

Replacements

Sometimes when things do not go well, people say, "Why don't we let others try it," as if a change in personnel is the best way to make improvements. When elected officials fail to fulfill their campaign promises, voters look to replace them in the next election. When bureaucrats are found to be incompetent, they are asked to hand in their resignations immediately. Even CEOs and general managers are not immune from the same fate when their performance does not meet company expectations.

Since replacements are readily available in every sector of society, people are used to the idea of changing jobs, cars, or houses whenever they feel like it. Some couples have even tested the limits of social conventions by exchanging partners. It seems like everything in this world, including organs and nationalities, can either be transplanted or replaced.

When we ask our friends or family to take our place in a losing game of poker, we are, in fact, trying to change our luck. When fans constantly harass the manager to bring in substitutes or umpires to change their calls, they themselves will be asked to either keep quiet or be removed from the stands. It is common for people to replace worn out furniture or a garment that is no longer fashionable. However, it is not normal for anyone to eat the same food everyday because a change in taste is natural. Even the way we think and the way we do things, such as how we sit, stand or sleep, needs a breath of fresh air every now and then.

Nevertheless, too much change is not a good thing, for it will create too many problems. For example, when a person has undergone more than one organ transplant in addition to an extensive cosmetic surgery, he/she will become an almost unrecognizable person whose old body has been torn apart and put back together with completely different parts.

If a new sports car does not have anything replaced for months and years, and ends up needing a major overhaul of all its parts, then it is probably already close to being on the way to a junkyard.

Although it is not a bad thing to replace the old with the new, it is not good to have frequent changes and replacements. Change does not necessarily mean progress. Sometimes, too many changes can bring about opposite effects. Nowadays, with all the advancements in agricultural technology, it is easier for farmers to replace old varieties when the size of the fruit grown is too small or when the rice harvest is not large enough. Some people are very eager to improve the quality of their offspring. It is rumored that some Japanese people are so tired of being short that they have invested a great deal in trying to make their children taller and stronger. Women all over the world go as far as to ask their doctors for the most intelligent and handsome sperm donors possible.

Some people prefer to have many honorary parents while neglecting to care for their own. It is even common for fraternal brothers to overlook the needs of their siblings. If a person finds nothing wrong in replacing his immediate family, it will not be a surprise when he/she changes nationality or last name.

Therefore, we should have the morals and character of an upright person. We must be able to make the right decision about what we need to change, and cherish what we have when the status quo is better.

Tending Life's Garden

A garden's trees and plants need water, fertilizer, and especially weeding and trimming. Tending a garden is important because when leaves and branches wither, they hamper growth if they are not pruned. For fruit trees, unhealthy and rotting fruit must be picked, or the rot will spread to the other fruit and ruin the crop.

Not only do we need to trim and cut plants and trees, our personal morals, speech, and behavior must also be trimmed of imperfections. For instance, when we are not knowledgeable, we should learn to enhance our learning. If we are inarticulate, we need to train ourselves in public speaking, and when we are lacking in capabilities, we must motivate ourselves to progress.

Women put on make-up in the morning to enhance their looks, and a warrior needs to fine-tune his swordsmanship to overcome all foes. Chefs must be particular about the ingredients of a gourmet dish, and writers of poetry and calligraphy need to produce numerous works before the best of their creations can be presented for the world to appreciate.

"Rid the decay and preserve the thriving" means we must correct our faults and cultivate merits. Otherwise, how are we going to improve? A pot of flowers must be trimmed in order to look its best, and our behavior needs to be refined before we can receive the praise of others.

When we have ulterior motives and expect a payback from others or some kind of award, we are creating decay in the course of practicing benevolence. On the other hand, when we are only filled with joy in doing good deeds, and have no intention of gaining recognition, we are nurturing our character.

No matter how beautiful a dress is, it loses its grace if it is stained. A garden of plum blossoms and lush willows will look forlorn if they are surrounded by withered branches and dead leaves. When our morals and character are flawed, we cannot win the respect of others no matter how great our achievements. Therefore, we should never stop tending to life's garden, trimming and ridding it of impurities and decaying matter. Only then will we be able to progress toward true benevolence, integrity, and beauty.

Life Skills Education

The most important thing in life is to get an education. There are many kinds of education: family, school, community, humanities, science, technology, arts, sports, ethics, and so forth, but the most important is life skills education.

What is life skills education? It is about daily necessities, such as clothing, food, shelter, and transportation. It covers activities like walking, sitting, standing, and resting; family life and filial ethics, socializing and interaction with people; speaking and conducting ourselves; and advancing or retreating in life. However, today's education mostly focuses on the transmission of knowledge and ignores an education in life skills. What a pity!

Today's high school and college graduates are for the most part considered well-educated, but if they were asked to prepare a cup of tea or sweep the floor, most would have no idea what to do. When guests arrive, they might not know how to make a simple snack or how to greet people properly.

Many of today's young people lack basic knowledge about their bodies and important health issues. They do not understand social etiquette and do not know how to deal with people. Their lack of life skills education is due to parents not teaching their children how to live, resulting in the latter only going through life watching television, playing video games, or getting on the Internet. They end up not knowing anything about living. Is this loving them or harming them? Indulging children with materialism seems to some parents an expression of love, but as these children grow up and enter the workforce without any life skills, parents will soon realize that they have in fact done a lot of harm!

Not only should parents teach their children basic cooking and cleaning skills, they should also show them how to survive under adverse circumstances such as unemployment, war, hurricanes, and earthquakes. These survival tactics are basic to living, and if there is no active education for such situations, how are children going to face crises in life later?

Regarding education, Confucianism teaches us to "Look upon no improper conduct, hear no improper speech, and speak no improper words." The son of Zhu Rongzhi, the Chinese premier, once picked something out of a garbage can. On hearing about it, Zhu told his son to take it back right away because "One should never take what is not given." This is education in living. Legend has it that George Washington chopped down a cherry tree. Though he made a mistake, by admitting his error, he was still commended by his parents. Woodrow Wilson braved a snowstorm and went to school carrying his books on his back. Even though it turned out that nobody else was there, the education he received from his parents was never to slack off in school.

Upon discovering that their children have offended the neighbors with what they have said, reasonable parents will take them over to apologize right away instead of protecting them. In educating children, we may give them a hard time temporarily, but that is to ensure the development of proper ethics and right thinking in the future. Nowadays, we advocate acquiring a better education for a better future, but in reality, every citizen should learn to apply higher standards to their lives in order to cultivate a well-rounded character. So life skills education is something we should really promote and emphasize!

Practical Knowledge

In everyday life, it may not be easy to detect a scholar, but it is easy to tell whether a person is knowledgeable in a practical sense.

People need to know about history, world geography, weather, and even different lifestyles and cultures. By looking at dark clouds in the sky, we know it will rain soon; by feeling a change in the wind, we know temperatures will drop. This knowledge helps us dress appropriately and protect ourselves from changing weather conditions.

We may not understand the Internet too well, but we should know how to use email. We may not be an expert on how the stock market works, but we ought to appreciate its relationship to the economy. We may not enjoy watching television or listening to the radio, but we surely need to know how to turn them on and off and how to use the remote controls, when necessary. We may not own a cell phone, but in case of an emergency we should know how to operate one. We need to have some basic knowledge about health, medicine, and even table manners. We should know procedures for meetings, etiquette for talking on the telephone, and conduct appropriate for air travel. In addition, we should be familiar with the meaning of the latest slang and acronyms.

There is an old Chinese saying, "Scholars need not leave their homes to know about what is happening in the world." But today, if we do not read a newspaper for a few days, we lose touch with the world. Common knowledge is so important for people!

When people socialize, they usually talk about the latest social trends. We need to know about these in order to participate. We need not be an expert on politics, economics, environmental protection, education, business, or technology, but we should keep ourselves informed. The average citizen these days must at least know how to file tax returns and complete the required forms while traveling abroad. Otherwise, it would be difficult to go anywhere. Life is not easy!

When we meet people from different walks of life, we should

know how to greet them. Living in a democratic country, we need to know what our civil rights are in elections, referendums, and public hearings. We should also have knowledge of the products we buy in terms of their functions, warranties, and return policies.

      The Buddha has ten titles of honor, and one of them is "All-Knowing One of the World." Even the Buddha had to understand how the world functioned. That is worldly knowledge. Today's life is difficult because we live in an age where there is a constant explosion of information. Everyday we see numerous changes of events, terms, laws, regulations, and knowledge. If we do not keep up with these changes, how can we handle life and society?

Conducting Ourselves

Is it really that difficult to conduct ourselves properly in life?

It is actually not that easy. Whenever we discuss with kindred minds the ways of learning or past and current issues, we might be filled with great enthusiasm and passion. When we exchange views with others on how to handle matters, even though we may have different opinions, theories, and approaches, we still usually feel a sense of excitement due to our mutual focus and seriousness. However, if we touch on the subject of how to conduct ourselves properly, we tend to be solemn and defensive, fearing what others say may hurt our feelings. We are reluctant to discuss our views and feelings even if we have some good thoughts to share, because we may not want to harm our relationships with those around us. When we cannot see eye to eye with others, relationships can become strained, and they may be difficult to repair later.

Disassociating ourselves from others does not help us become better people, improve our speech, or ensure that we walk our path in life smoothly. We need training and guidance in the skills we acquire in order to make a living, work, and get things done. We take lessons in painting, music, gardening, and general administration in order to live more fulfilled and successful lives. However, our morals, human relations, integrity, and virtues also need to be strengthened over time. If we do not study and reflect on how to conduct ourselves, how can we expect to learn to do so properly?

Parents love and protect their children, but love and protection alone do not necessarily make people good. Teachers educate their students, but their teaching may not result in good people. People are not born with knowledge; they need to learn before they can acquire it.

Humans are indeed unpredictable and diverse beings. Some people are happy to hear about their mistakes, while others are filled with contempt. Some people are always humble, always reminding themselves of their imperfections. Other people think of all the different ways they can show off their greatness and prominence. Some people always feel that their morals and self-cultivation are not good enough. When they feel ashamed of their inadequacies, they vow to change and improve. On the other hand, some people love to narrate stories of old glory, and of unreachable dreams for the future and their incredible strengths.

There are people who like to praise, respect, and speak well of others. Then there are those who only enjoy praising themselves and showing off their merits. Some people believe that others are bad while they are good. However, some people may observe themselves, realize their own shortcomings, and come to the conclusion that others are right.

There are so many different ways of conducting oneself. Wise reader, how do you want to conduct yourself in life?

Body Language

When legislators in Taiwan debate and argue during their meetings, sometimes blows fly instead of words when they scuffle. The media euphemistically calls this "body language." It is unfortunate that conflicts and fistfights are termed as such. Body language more aptly refers to gestures, expressions, and the postures a speaker makes in order to highlight a point and to improve the effect of spoken words.

There are other kinds of body language. In commercials we often see an athlete with a strong physique drinking Gatorade and punching the air with his/her fists as a sign of physical strength. When election results are counted, winning candidates are seen surrounded by supporters flashing the victory sign. During a lecture, the speaker may shrug his/her shoulders to show helplessness. We may point to our eyes to indicate careful inspection, beat our chests to express anguish, and push away with our hands to convey refusal. These are all examples of body language.

In a religious context, body language should express kind hearts and good wishes. In Buddhism, we join palms, do a half bow, prostrate ourselves, circumambulate, and make different hand gestures as a sign of respect and courtesy to others. Furthermore, we are instructed to "walk like the wind, stand like a pine, sit like a bell, and lie like a bow," all the basic postures of a practitioner. Especially interesting is the body language of Chan masters. Once when asked what is the Way, a master replied by sticking up his index finger. When asked what is the meaning of the First Patriarch coming to the west, he shook his duster. When asked what was our true face before our parents gave birth to us, he drew a large circle in the air. The Buddha famously held up a flower in his hand to convey the Dharma to his disciple Mahakasyapa. Images of the Avalokitesvara Bodhisattva holding a willow twig convey his compassion in helping all sentient beings. Those of the Amitabha Buddha have open hands reaching down to signify receiving people to his Pure Land,

and the Manjusri Bodhisattva crosses his legs to show his ease.

Other religions and cultures employ symbolic body language, too. Nowadays, Catholics kiss the ring of the Pope. Followers of Jesus kissed his feet. Eastern and Western cultures also have different social mores and etiquette. People may raise their hats, shake hands, hug, kiss the cheeks, and touch faces or noses to show friendliness and affection. Sometimes customs are considered strange and are difficult to accept by those from a different culture. For example, the indigenous tribes in Taiwan hook their legs together to indicate joy in being with someone, clap each other's hands for comradeship, and applaud to welcome visitors. They also draw many pictures and signs on their bodies as symbols of beauty and courage.

There are so many kinds of body language. Those who cannot hear use sign language to communicate. In dancing, acrobatics, and martial arts, practitioners exhibit graceful body language. Some young men and women use eye contact and smiles to convey their affection for one another. Little children hide behind their mothers when they are shy, and their mothers may stare at them with disapproval when they misbehave. Even animals use body language. In one story, a mother goose pecked on the pant leg of a police officer to get help for her baby.

Regardless of what gestures we make, there is always expression and substance within our body language that can be extended to others. However, it is disgraceful to call kicking and punching body language. The media should be more circumspect in the language it uses.

Poise

There are many occasions in life in which people are defeated in a competition. They lose elections, games of bridge, and sports events. However, even in defeat, they never lose their poise. In a basketball game, once a foul is called by the referee, a player will put up his/her hands to admit fault. Tennis players always shake hands after a match to exhibit their poise and etiquette.

When we behave well and do not bicker with others over small things, we are showing poise. Politicians, athletes, and scholars all have their own respective etiquette. A professor once brought his son along with him to shop for fruit. As he was carefully selecting the fruit, the storekeeper got impatient with him and asked, "Do you really want to buy some fruit or not?"

The professor replied, "Yes, yes!" and continued to look at the fruit.

After a while the storekeeper could not stand it anymore and said rudely, "Stop picking around! You're not going to buy anyway."

The professor politely explained, "Oh yes, of course I'm going to buy some." Later on he chose some fruit and paid for it.

On their way home, his son looked unhappy, and his father asked him, "Why do you seem upset?"

The son answered, "I'm really ashamed of you, dad. You're a professor and yet you let a fruit vendor scold you. What an insult!"

His father consoled his son, "Son, don't be angry. That is exactly why I am a scholar and a professor." The poise of a scholar is not something everyone has.

Poise was a category first used during the Wei-Jin Dynasties for critiquing people's literary eloquence, but later it was also used for judging the spirit and character of noted personalities. Poise is the result of cultivation, respect, and tolerance. People who are learned and have a good grasp of reasoning usually are poised and respectful.

The mayor of Kaohsiung, Taiwan put it well: "A democracy should have order, tolerance, and poise." During a presidential election in America, the first thing the losing candidate does is to show poise and politeness by congratulating the winner. Englishmen are often considered gentlemen with good manners, while Buddhists are often praised for being the most spiritually poised. A famed general of the Epoch of the Warring States once wrote, "When the wise break up a friendship, they do not say anything negative about the other. When loyal ministers leave their country, they do not try to preserve their reputation at the expense of their nation." Venerable Master Xuanzang, demonstrating the poise of a cultivated practitioner, was described as one who practiced "no utterance of fame or fortune, no behavior of vanity or impracticality."

Once a man went to the house of Shi Manqing, a Song Dynasty scholar, claiming the cow Shi had in his house was actually the same one he had lost. Shi simply replied, "Since it is the one you lost, just take it home with you." Later, the man discovered that he had made a mistake. He returned the cow and apologized deeply. Shi said, "People make mistakes sometimes. What's past is past; you don't have to apologize." Shi's tolerance and poise are in character with that of being a scholar.

However, people in all professions should be poised. Men, women, young, and old should have individual deportment, and the same goes for lovers in love. Even in playing a game of chess, both those playing and watching should be aware of proper manners. As the saying goes, "The truly virtuous are those who can watch a chess game without commenting. The truly brave are those who never renege after making a move."

As humans, we should be poised to earn the respect and appreciation of others. Whether we are rich or poor, noble or common, wise or ignorant, we are all subject to losing at times. However, we should never lose our poise!

Sportsmanship

Playing sports is not only good for one's health, but also one's behavior. Since nobody is perfect, sports offer us the opportunity to better ourselves both ethically and morally. Basketball, for example, can offer many valuable lessons about life. The following is a list of principles we can learn just from the game of basketball:

1. People have a strong tendency to ignore their own mistakes, but on a basketball court nothing escapes the watchful eyes of the referee. Once his whistle blows, the offending player must immediately raise his hand and acknowledge the fact that he has committed a foul. There is nothing anyone can say or do to change the situation.
2. Although basketball is a game of intensity and physical contact, in accordance with the established rules, fouls are not allowed. Blocking, charging, illegal hand-checks, and reach-ins are fouls that are always counted personally against the players. When a serious foul is committed, apologies are often expected from the offender.
3. Basketball is the perfect training ground for quickness and agility. If a player is hesitant in making decisions, he/she will never know when it is the right time to pass or shoot the ball. When scoring opportunities are constantly missed because of a player's indecisiveness, the coach will have no choice but to make a substitution.
4. Basketball is definitely a team sport and not an individual contest to see who can score the most points. All five players on the court must play as a team if they want to win the game. If a player is selfish and refuses to pass the ball, he will find a permanent seat on the bench.
5. In team competition, it is very easy for players to have a sense of honor and dignity. If a player is without the necessary

fighting spirit, he/she will never become a true athlete. However, if a player gives all his/her effort regardless of the outcome of the game, he/she will earn the praise of those people watching and playing with him/her.

6. Although competition can be fierce and intense, players should never have disrespect for their opponents. They must be tolerant as well as grateful for the opportunity to compete and learn.

Today, much emphasis is placed on the development of student athletes in our schools. Students are not only given the opportunity to learn in a classroom setting but also a chance to participate in sports so they can understand the meaning of teamwork and the importance of sportsmanship. Accordingly, sports are inherently an education on the values of courage, wisdom, and compassion in life. If we want to be physically strong and mentally tough, we might as well start our training on a basketball court.

The Importance of Expressions

People are creatures of expression and emotion. Through our facial expressions, others know what is on our minds. Even without showing anger or joy on our faces, our tone of voice and body language can reveal to others what we are thinking.

However, some people neither gesture nor speak. Their stony faces betray no sign of life at all. Though they are alive, others might as well take them as dead. People describe individuals without expression, voice, or gestures as zombies or the living dead. Their lives are utterly lifeless. Their sad state is so unfortunate that even heaven and earth feel sorry for them!

In the circus, clowns act funny to win the laughter of the audience. But if we respond without expression, speech, or applause, we are no better than the clowns. Even toddlers learn to please the grown-ups around them with a cute move or a funny face. Can we not do better ourselves? When we are filled with inhibitions, our wooden faces are so forbidding that it looks as if the whole world has wronged us and owes us a great deal. Paying back others' enthusiasm with a cold shoulder is very cruel indeed.

We live in a world of sounds. So we need to speak up loudly. This is the age of colors. So we need to smile, for smiles are colorful. This is also the age of motion. So we need to be active to show others that we are alive.

The Discourses of the Buddha [*Agama Sutras*] state that there are five kinds of inhumanity:

1. When a person ought to be compassionate, he/she is not.
2. When a person ought to feel joy, he/she does not.
3. When a person ought to speak, he/she does not.
4. When a person should be moved, he/she feels nothing.
5. When a person should be active, he/she is not.

Even the Buddha was helpless when faced with such inhumanity.

When we see a cat, it meows at us. When we come across a dog, it wags its tail. According to some research, even plants grow better and flowers bloom prettier when talked to and praised. They display the best of their beauty to repay the attention they receive. As humans, how can we afford to be without expression?

Facial expressions are very important. The expression of the Buddha is always one of compassion. That of bodhisattvas is intimate and warm. Arhats also carry a countenance of wisdom. Even ascetic monks have expressions. Theirs is one of making vows. When the modern scholar, Hu Shi, was teaching others how to write, he said, "A good piece of writing expresses feelings and emotions. When both are well-expressed, it is excellent writing."

For those who have no expression, please smile, talk, and feel the joy of life, for your own sake as well as for that of others.

Cryonics

Nowadays, some people feel so unhappy with their lives that they want to make use of science to freeze and store their bodies so that they can live a different life thirty or fifty years later. In reality, if we think a little deeper, our parents and friends might all be gone thirty or fifty years from now. When the people we are used to being around are gone and our habits are no longer the same as everyone else's, what fun will it be if we live again?

Cryonics may be justified in some cases for medical reasons. For example, people with Lou Gehrig's disease lose the use of their muscles and speech over time. In the end they need the support of medical equipment even to breathe. When a person cannot speak, walk, move his/her arms, or express him/herself in any manner, life can feel worse than death.

Yet some people who are unhappy with life and want their bodies to be cryonically frozen are still healthy physically and mentally. Then, there are those whose facial expressions or mentality are already similar to that of a cryonic body. It is certainly not something to be desired.

When we look at faces in a crowd these days, there are so many walking around with long faces, unable to smile. It seems that either the whole world has let them down or someone has seriously offended them. Some people either say very little or they do not speak well. They should realize that a canary that does not sing may very well end up as a bird in the oven for dinner. These people may have their own way of thinking, but it is narrow. Their minds lack empathy, and they treat people with coldness and indifference. Although such people are alive, they are more like walking corpses or cryonic beings.

In *The Discourses of the Buddha*, the Buddha spoke about five kinds of "non-humans." They are those who do not speak, laugh, or act when they should; they are not joyous when they should be or do not praise others accordingly. These "non-humans" are similar to cryonic bodies.

Modern people drive for convenience and efficiency, but if there are no cars available, they do not want to walk to get things done. Our hands can do a lot of work. However, when people get used to doing everything with a remote control, they no longer know what to do with their hands without it. We should speak with our mouths, but we have learned to rely on microphones, and some people refuse to talk without one. We wear glasses to help us see, but many people will not even try to see without them. These trends do not simply mean we are advancing materially. Instead, we have become too reliant on these so-called advances and have allowed ourselves to degenerate. In the end, we turn ourselves into a kind of cryonic automaton.

When the diplomatic relationship between two countries deteriorates and becomes frozen, a good mediator is capable of thawing it out. If there is animosity between two friends, a common friend can help them resolve it and warm things up again. So, how are we going to thaw our own faults, shortcomings, and apathy to avoid becoming cryonic beings?

Two-Faced People

Credibility is not a characteristic of two-faced people because it is not a trademark of the unprincipled. Those with two faces have no concept of right and wrong, or loyalty and betrayal. They go or act whichever way the wind blows.

Two-faced people are also hypocrites who will cry with one eye and laugh with the other. They are like two-headed snakes that will do anything to please either of the two contending sides, or sow the seeds of discord among amicable parties. They have a vagueness about them because whatever they say cannot be taken at face value. They are also double-talkers who can say one thing and mean something else. Two-faced people are nothing like the ancient warriors and strategists who were firmly loyal to their masters. Although they resorted to ruses to protect their lords or win battles, they would have never sacrificed their principles. Because of their determination and unwavering character, they had much greater dignity than the two-faced person straddling the fence. There are undoubtedly good and bad people in this world. The good will act and speak with morality and benevolence, while the bad will cheat, lie, and steal without conscience. If those who are bad happen to do something right, it is because they have stumbled upon it. Although their actions are undesirable and at times harmful, they are still a step above the deeds of two-faced people.

A kind or mean person is easy to gauge as long as he/she is frank and straightforward. On the other hand, two-faced people are hard to judge because they can be hypocritical and malevolent at the same time. They can lure unsuspecting victims into their traps with a kind face and sweet talk. However, no matter how good their acts may be, they soon run out of disguises and reveal their true colors if they carry on with their double-crossing ways. People will come to despise them for what they are.

There are some people who can speak as the occasion dictates, because they are well versed in the ways of the world. Although they are worldly people, they do not have two faces. Two-faced people can be a sheep on the outside and a wolf on the inside. They can be mean and vicious with their words and deeds, but in actuality, they are just putting on airs to scare off the good and the virtuous. The worst thing about those people who have two faces is their elusiveness. They hide their true nature. They rarely speak their minds, but will do anything to cover their tracks. They can praise you in your face and later criticize you behind your back. Just when you think they are trustworthy, they might do something to hurt you.

  Over the ages, there have been many people who have hidden their deceit behind a mask of friendship or tender loving care. They have pretended to love, respect, or protect someone while plotting his/her death. Although we are fearful of bad people and the things they are capable of doing, we know what and who they are. However, we cannot say the same thing about two-faced people, because we are surprised when they double-cross us. We often see them as good people and inadvertently put ourselves in harm's way. Therefore, they are even more fearful than bad people.

To Walk in Another's Shoes

When we praise someone for being an understanding person, he/she will be pleased with the compliment. A great part of our humanity actually lies in our ability to understand the thoughts and feelings not only of others, but also of nature and the material world. It allows us to respect and accept the ways of others and the course of nature.

In order to be understanding, we must be fully aware of what others are feeling. We must know a grudge when we see one and never wear out our welcome. If we are to have close friends, we must be empathetic of their views and never turn their goodwill into malice, or misconstrue their kindness as pretension.

As for the forces of nature, if we do not appreciate their unpredictability, we may suffer great losses both physically and financially. Moreover, if we do not know anything about our material world, our lives will be incomplete. For example, we would be at a loss in today's world if we did not know how to turn on a computer, send an email, drive a car, or use a cell phone. We can become frustrated if we do not know how to change a light bulb or maintain a garden. Even our pets are good at understanding our wants and needs. Therefore, we must return the favor by knowing when they are hungry, thirsty, or playful, and when they need our tender loving care.

Although people have a lot to learn in this world, what we need to know the most are the thoughts and feelings of others. Yet often this turns out to be the most difficult lesson. As a saying goes, "You may know a person by his/her face, but you cannot read his/her mind." Even if we know people's names or their achievements, we really know very little about them if we do not walk a mile in their shoes.

In society, there are many bosses who are very good at "recognizing a person." They are experts in judging a person's talent and employing it in the best way possible. How then do we know if a person is loyal or disloyal, good or bad, moral or immoral, capable or incapable?

Sometimes, we can know people by their facial expressions, the way they speak, and how they treat or get along with others. We can also know people by their thoughts and feelings.

According to the *Diamond Sutra* [*Vajracchedika-prajnaparamita Sutra*], there are many different kinds of living beings and many different kinds of minds, but the Buddha sees and knows them all. This is what allows the Buddha and bodhisattvas to impart their teachings in accordance with the variance in situations and the listeners' dispositions. Not only do they recognize people's characteristics, but they also understand their true nature. Similarly, if spouses are to strengthen their understanding of each other, they must have trust in one another. If parents are to maintain a healthy relationship with their children, they must be aware of what is on their children's minds, recognize their needs, and know their friends.

To know a person well is a monumental task that is not easy for anyone to accomplish. However, if we can empathize with what others are thinking, we will have no problem knowing them well. All the great rulers of the past and the successful leaders of the present were able to achieve what they did because of the advantage of knowing what people need. On the other hand, some people often complain about being misled by friends, betrayed by colleagues, or fired from their jobs. It is quite possible that all this is due to them not being understanding or considerate of the needs of others.

Understanding other people's thoughts and feelings is a profound subject that can only be acquired from personal experience, and not from intelligence and knowledge. Being understanding and considerate of others requires tremendous effort on our part before we can truly know what it is like to walk in another's shoes.

Likes and Dislikes

In this world, there are things that we like and dislike. Sometimes, there are deeds we know are good, but we are unwilling to do them, because we dislike doing them. There are also deeds we know are harmful, but we do them anyway, because they give us momentary pleasure. However, we cannot base our actions on likes and dislikes. If something ought to be done, we must do it regardless of what we enjoy. If something should not to be done, we should not forge ahead.

Since true happiness lies in helping others, we should enjoy helping others even if it is something we initially do not like to do. It is important for us to realize that likes and dislikes should not dictate our actions. We should, instead, make ourselves do what is right and avoid what is wrong. Our decisions should not involve personal feelings. If our country were to be invaded by another country, we must be willing to sacrifice our lives to protect our nation. No one wants to risk dying in battle, but if it is our duty to serve our country in times of need, we must do so.

We all love money, and most of us would like to be millionaires. However, not everyone can win the lottery or make a fortune. We should therefore not waste energy daydreaming about it. Even though we may not be naturally inclined to do so, we should focus instead on giving what we can to the needy and not be miserly in supporting a worthy cause. Otherwise, our stinginess will ruin our reputation, honor, and even friendships. We must try our best to lend a helping hand in any way we can.

There is a popular saying today, "As long as I like it, there is nothing that I cannot do." This kind of thinking is not only dangerous, but will also lead to destructive behaviors. We cannot simply follow our desires and only do the things that we like. We must have consideration for others' feelings and not do things that will cause them pain and suffering. In other words, we must not breach the rules of morality.

Therefore, instead of doing things that only please us, we should please others as well.

While some people are very devoted to the interest of their communities, others have no intention of getting involved. No matter how we feel about our community, being a member of it makes us responsible for its welfare. The same goes for our friends and families. Some of us might not be close to our relatives and may not even like them very much, but we still need to answer their calls for help. Someday, we might need them as well.

Although there is no harm in having fun and enjoying life, we must not offend public decency in our pursuit of happiness. We must be careful in choosing our friends by staying away from those who are corrupt and immoral. We must constantly remind ourselves to say no to bad habits such as drinking and gambling. These are all things we should dislike.

In reality, we do not have much choice in what we like or dislike. We must bring ourselves to like things that are good for others, because we must care about what benefits society in general. We must also learn to distance ourselves from things that are harmful to others. Since all our actions affect others, our likes and dislikes should never be determined merely by personal feelings.

Our personal happiness and pleasure should therefore never be the main motivation for our actions. We must strive to bring joy and happiness to the greatest number of people. If we want others to accept us, we must consider the interests of others in determining our likes and dislikes. We cannot just go our own way without any regard for how others feel, because it is the public, as well as the Law of Cause and Effect, that should govern and determine our actions.

All in all, we should be very careful in what we like and do not like, and in what we should and should not do.

The Art of Refusing

Have you ever been refused something? How did you feel at that time? Did you feel uncomfortable or embarrassed? A good supervisor or a capable person would not refuse a request easily. When they do so, they generally offer something else as an alternative. We all need to learn the art of refusal.

When we make a request or discuss something with others, if they are enthusiastic and positive in their response, we feel happy. However, if they are reluctant and difficult, coming up with many excuses to put us off, we will surely consider them stubborn, inconsiderate, and hard to work with.

When the average citizen goes to government agencies to request documents or to settle personal affairs, often they are met by bureaucrats who frustrate him/her with red tape in order to exert their authority. Thus, government agencies are often viewed as removed and unreasonable by its citizens.

We should learn the art of refusal because rejection can be very demoralizing to bear. This art involves not refusing outright, not refusing easily, and not refusing when we are angry. We should never refuse casually, coldly, or arrogantly.

If refusal is the only option, we still need to respect others' feelings. We should speak gently with a good attitude and smile so that the other person can appreciate our sincerity and good intentions. In addition, when refusing others, we should provide an alternative to their request. Suppose a subordinate asks for an air-conditioner. If we cannot oblige, we should at least give him/her an electric fan. If a friend wants roses and we cannot afford or find them, we should maybe offer carnations in their place. When we have to refuse others but at the same time we provide them with a practical alternative, they will surely understand our goodwill.

In human relations, if we can show others more consideration, latitude, tolerance, convenience, less rejection, and less embarrassment, we will surely win their support. On the other hand, if we easily reject our conditions and opportunities with others, then little by little we will lose their respect, trust, and friendship. Therefore, we should not reject others easily. Instead, if we follow our causes and conditions with an open mind, then we can find more opportunities to learn and develop. By giving others more positive causes and conditions, we benefit ourselves even more.

Not Going Against Another's Wishes

Humans are social animals. Yet how can we best be accepted by our peers in our daily interactions with others? First, we must be flexible in accepting another's opinion. We cannot always think that we are right and others wrong. Most importantly, we must not be overly subjective and selfish in our intentions. We must put ourselves in others' shoes, even when making decisions that have only a slight impact on them. Only then will we be accepted and welcomed by those around us, and be a positive influence. "To comply with the wishes of every living being" is one of the Ten Vows of the Samantabhadra Bodhisattva. It is a vow that places great emphasis on the interests of the public. Simply put, it entails not going against another's wishes.

To comply with another's wishes is not the same as to cater blindly to another's wants or to use excess flattery. It is using compassion and wisdom to interact with our fellow human beings, relying on skill to achieve harmonious relationships, and establishing good affinities and long-lasting friendships with others. The Buddhist principle of "teaching in accordance with one's temperament and adapting to others through common interests," along with the Confucian teaching of "teaching without regard to one's upbringing, but in accordance with one's aptitude" are both ways of transforming the world through loving-kindness and compassion. Without taking into account the needs and circumstances of others, it is not possible to teach the Dharma effectively.

To comply with another's wishes is to willingly follow what is right in the pursuit of truth, goodness, and beauty without any hint of self-attachment. It is to help others without regret or expectation. It is saying "ok" more often than saying "no." If a refusal is unavoidable, an alternative should be offered to resolve the problem.

Not going against another's wishes also means being respectful and magnanimous toward others in all aspects of life. For example, not going against one's parents is pious, while not always going against one's children is open-minded. Not going against one's superior is obedient, while not going against one's subordinate is respectful. Not going against one's friend is to cultivate a close and intimate friendship. If we can learn to properly comply with another's wishes, we will have the ability to manage our affairs and deal with others harmoniously.

Nowadays, people often neglect each other's needs. What we should do is cultivate our ability to comply with the wishes of others. Not going against the wishes of others is the highest practice and the noblest character anyone can have. Subhuti, one of the Buddha's chief disciples and the foremost in understanding the Doctrine of Sunyata (Emptiness), had the utmost respect for the Buddha. His compliance with the Buddha's wishes can best be described as "if the Buddha wanted him to stand, he dared not sit; if the Buddha wanted him to sit, he dared not stand." Furthermore, when the Buddha himself was a young prince in a previous life, he would give up anything in his possession that was asked of him, including his belongings, his wealth, his palace, and even his wife and children. Therefore, he was also known as "The Prince of Perfect Giving." Likewise, many eminent masters of Buddhism have done what others could not, such as "letting spit dry on one's face" or "purposely degrading one's own abilities."

Those who are able to comply with another's wishes will be successful in whatever they do. But those who insist on being disagreeable will not receive much help in their endeavors. If government officials keep in mind the needs of the people and make decisions accordingly, they will be loved and praised as honest officials. If Buddhist practitioners abide by the principle of "never seeking pleasure for oneself, but always vowing to deliver all beings from the endless cycles of suffering," they will achieve enlightenment and have the highest virtue. Not going against another's wishes is indeed the highest wisdom we can have in dealing with worldly affairs and the noblest way to interact with others.

Sandwich Cookie

Sandwich cookies have become very popular because they can have different fillings in the center. They can be light but also satisfying. However, in life people find it difficult being sandwiched between two bigger or stronger sides. For instance, when parents fight, their children are sandwiched between them not knowing whether they should take the side of their father or mother.

Within a family, the relationship between in-laws can be strained at times, especially between a mother- and daughter-in-law. In the old days, Chinese men sometimes had more than one wife, and the wives might not have been on the best of terms with each other. Men often found themselves stuck in the middle of both situations. However, while problems between in-laws are often inevitable, men in the past only had themselves to blame when they got stuck between quarreling wives. Qing Emperor Guang Xu was a pitiful emperor because he was caught between the Empress Dowager and his favorite concubine. He never dared to take a stand. He was truly a "sandwich cookie" with little to relish. Nowadays in society, there are many examples of people in a similar plight of not knowing which side they should lean toward. In public office, it seems that the best positions are those at the top or down at the bottom. Those people sandwiched in middle management often find themselves having a hard time pleasing their bosses and trying not to upset their subordinates at the same time.

Besides personal and work relationships, countries also face similar predicaments. The smaller nations in Europe often find themselves stuck between the superpowers not knowing which side to support. When the U.S. and the Soviet Union were the world's two sole superpowers during the Cold War, many countries around the world became sandwiched between them and found it difficult to pick one side over the other.

A fifth of the population in Singapore is Malaysian. If one day there is war between Singapore and Malaysia, what would these Malaysians who are also Singaporean citizens do? In Taiwan, there are almost four million people who consider themselves originally from Mainland China. If China invades Taiwan some day, these Chinese "sandwich cookies" will have a very hard time.

If we have indeed become a sandwich cookie, we need to resolve the situation. A man became stuck between his fighting mother and wife and did not know what he should do. He was inspired one day and told his mother he would divorce his wife in half a year and pleaded with her to tolerate her daughter-in-law. He then told his wife they would move to another place in six months and asked her to do her best to show his mother love and care. Half a year later, his mother could not bear to see her daughter-in-law leave, and his wife did not want to move out.

The center of a sandwich is for balance and is what makes it taste good. Therefore, those who find themselves sandwiched in the middle should use their wisdom to avoid offending either side. This way, they will be able to savor the best of both worlds, while still making everyone happy.

Understanding the Greater Good

Since a nation represents the "collective" of its people, individuals should never compromise its reputation and honor for the sake of personal gain or interests. Instead, every citizen needs to appreciate the meaning of the "greater good."

Aside from the interests of the nation, people should also take into consideration the interests of their organizations, employers, superiors, and associates. They should never dismiss or discriminate against them due to personal disagreements. Instead they need to keep the "greater good" in mind. Although everyone has the right to pursue his/her own interests, people who understand "the greater good" will never try to profit at the expense of others, especially their friends and families.

By contrast, people who do not understand the meaning of the "greater good" will go to any length to fulfill their own selfish interests. They make false accusations or bring unfounded lawsuits against those who are close to them. They will not hesitate to hurt those who have benefited them and will do anything to advance their personal goals. People without a sense of the "greater good" sign their own death warrants, because they do not understand the meaning of "When natural disaster strikes, we can overcome it; but if we create bad karma, we dig our own graves." In other words, such people not only injure others in the pursuit of self-interest, but also harm themselves. When they choose to betray or harm others just to gain a quick advantage, their conduct and character will ultimately end up being shunned by the world.

People without regard for the collective are petty and untrustworthy. Although they may not realize their own faults, others will know them well through their words and deeds. In talking with others, they tend to betray their friends and those who have given them support. They are also often full of complaints, criticisms, and gossip, acting as if the whole world has been unjust to them. In reality, their behavior is similar to offering others an inappropriate gift. When it is not accepted, the giver will have to take it back.

People who do not understand the "greater good" quarrel easily with friends over trivial matters. In doing business, when they hear opinions that are different from their own, they will boycott their partners. They scheme and plot to disrupt a good project or a profitable venture. By doing so, they not only sacrifice other people's interests, but also their own. People are truly ignorant of the "greater good" when they do not care for the interests of their parents, teachers, friends, or subordinates.

Some of these people are even capable of committing treason against their own country. Although they may be shrewd and calculating, they will always be traitors in the eyes of their countrymen. For example, Benedict Arnold's plan to surrender West Point to the British during the American Revolution made his name synonymous with treachery. Robert Hanson's spying for the former Soviet Union earned him the tag of one who is willing to trade loyalty for money. On the other hand, there are intelligence agents who would rather die than give up any information even when the enemy catches them. They are indeed people who understand the meaning of the "greater good."

When Venerable Shuangting was to become the abbot of Jinshan Temple in the early 1900s, his senior Dharma brother Master Zongyang made a surprise return. His unexpected arrival led many to speculate that it was Zongyang's intention to compete for the abbotship. In order to put everyone's mind at ease, the Master wrote a congratulatory poem to Shuangting to reassure everyone that he had no such ambition. Upon learning of his virtuous act, everybody praised Zongyang as a man of high principles, who understood the meaning of the "greater good."

We all need to cultivate a sense of the "greater good" in order to conduct ourselves properly with dignity and morality, and to be like the pine and cypress, withstanding the cold frost and icy snow of life.

Good, Yet Useless People

We generally categorize people as good or bad. However, there are bad people among the good and vice versa. For instance, Robin Hood was a robber who benefited the poor and needy. He was a good example of someone who was bad and good at the same time.

Good people should be praised and admired. However, there is a type of good person who can be regarded as "useless," because they cannot accomplish anything positive and often succeed in spoiling matters instead. They are weak, indecisive, confused, and have no views on anything. They not only fail to protect the organizations they belong to, but also never provide benefits. However, because they do not cause any harm to others, are conciliatory in face of conflicts, and work quietly in their jobs, we consider them as good, yet useless.

We often hear people mention "so and so" is a good person. However, does he/she have the qualifications to be such? He/she should be compassionate in upholding morals, gregarious at work, progressive and diligent in serving others, and generous with his/her skills. When he/she has all those qualities and conducts him/herself well on all occasions, he/she is more than a good person. He/she is also a very capable person. On the other hand, if someone shirks responsibility, does not hold any views, is always fearful, and is only interested in protecting his/her position without the courage to report on evil, he/she is labeled a good, yet useless person. People who do not stand up for what they believe in when they should are not truly good. They are the stumbling blocks to an organization's growth, obstacles to society, and an impending crisis for the country's welfare.

The following are qualities of truly good, useful people:
1. *Compassion:* Compassion should not be excessive or abused. For instance, being compassionate to harmful people or providing hideouts for criminals on the run is being cruel to the general public. Therefore, good people should have wise and

courageous compassion.
2. *Diligence:* Diligence does not include loitering, having fun, gossiping, or creating problems for the world. It should be right diligence in serving others, personal cultivation, and taking up the right causes.
3. *Courage:* Courage is not reckless bravado that lacks planning, takes advantage of the weak, or seeks pleasure in fighting. Courage requires compassion and righteousness. It is being willing to shoulder responsibility and to remain open and progressive.
4. *Reasoning:* Reasoning does not mean being argumentative or outwitting others in a debate. If a person is only good at talking and not getting anything done, what good is that? Rather, reasoning refers to going with what is benevolent and making good connections with others. The key to good reasoning is being strict with oneself and being magnanimous when dealing with others.

Who are good people and who are bad ones? It is not easy to tell on the surface. There are people who appear benevolent but actually have the "happy face of Maitreya and the heart of a venomous serpent." These people are more fearful than bad ones. On the other hand, there are people who seem bad, but they are similar to robbers who have morals, like Robin Hood. Therefore, a rough, rude person who lends a helping hand in the face of injustice is a better person than a useless one.

Helping Others Succeed

In *Liao Fan's Four Lessons* [*Liaofan Sixun*], it is mentioned that people should make use of every opportunity in life to practice benevolence, and one of the ten ways to do so is to help others succeed. Benefiting others is a virtue. We can do so by providing others assistance in what they do, saying a few good words about them or providing them with positive conditions.

When we single out someone as noble, it is often because he/she has a big heart in helping others succeed. On the contrary, those who are petty will not help others gain success. They may also be jealous, cause trouble, or even stab others in the back.

In 1969, two astronauts, Neil Armstrong and Edwin Aldrin, landed on the moon. However, nowadays most people only know about Armstrong and very few about Aldrin. The reason is, of course, Armstrong was the first person to step on the moon, and his words, "One small step for man, one giant leap for mankind," have become world famous. The fact that Aldrin also landed on the moon is forgotten. On their return to Earth, a reporter asked Aldrin, "Neil Armstrong stepped out of the spaceship first to become the first man on the moon. Do you have any regrets?" Instead of being envious, Aldrin was very gracious in his response: "Don't forget that when we came back to Earth, I stepped out first so I was the first person to return to Earth from the moon."

During the Jin Dynasty, there was a minister named Qi Huangyang. Once, the emperor asked him to recommend someone to be county magistrate. Qi suggested his enemy. The emperor was surprised. To that, Qi replied, "You only asked me for a county magistrate and not who my enemy is." Later, when a military position became vacant, the emperor asked him for another recommendation. This time, Qi recommended his own son. Again, the emperor was surprised. Qi explained, "You only asked me for a military official and not who my son is." Qi made his recommendations for his country, not based on jealousy toward his enemy, or because of his family ties. Aside from being impartial, he also had the intention to help others succeed.

In assisting others to succeed, we need to have respect for others while being humble ourselves. We should not be calculating, but instead we should treat others as we would ourselves. Organ donation nowadays is a perfect example. Another good example is when only those with merit are recommended for public office. In Buddhism, making a connection, taking joy in others' benevolence, and saying a word of blessing or encouragement are all ways to help others.

We do not necessarily have to be the one to succeed, because when others do, we can still feel honored on their behalf. After all, when we help others fulfill their goals, we also share in their glory. Then, why is it that we do not always do so?

To Perform

Starting from birth, we have been "performing" constantly all our lives. Children cry in order to get what they want, and young people show off their courage, passion, and energy. In reaching adulthood, we demonstrate to others our wisdom, capabilities, and achievements. Some people display their wealth as symbols of power and status, or their poise as a sign of maturity. There are people who exhibit their goodness with ethics, or who use intelligence and wisdom to distinguish themselves. Men put on a smart suit and tie to show off their good looks, and women use make-up to flaunt their beauty.

People in different professions all need to perform to the best of their abilities. For instance, to show others what they are good at singers use their voices, athletes demonstrate their physical prowess, chefs use their cooking expertise, speakers move us with their eloquence, scientists publish their research findings, entrepreneurs produce quality products, warriors wield their weapons, and writers intrigue us with their creativity.

Colleges and universities accept students based on test results. Their scores are the basis for acceptance into any institution or course of study. Corporations hire people with the right abilities and skills. Airlines hire people with poise and elegance as flight attendants because those two qualities are fundamental to performing their jobs. Bus drivers need to be punctual and keep their schedules. The highest achievement in doing business is demonstrating credibility. Workers and farmers use diligence in proving their production targets. Teachers have to speak well and be creative in the ways they teach. Religious leaders teach the truth to benefit all sentient beings in order to convey their compassion.

Nature is also good at displaying its special characteristics. Blooming flowers show off their color; lush green mountains impose their magnificence; tall trees show their grandeur; the sun, moon, and stars glimmer brightly; the blue sky and azure ocean sparkle with depth and breadth; and trickling brooks and streams flow far and wide.

Animals are good performers as well. Peacocks spread their tail feathers to exhibit their elegance, spiders knit webs to show their perseverance, dolphins perform tricks to display their skills, while parrots talk to demonstrate their ability to imitate. Lions roar ferociously, ants gather food and bees produce honey industriously, dogs wag their tails with devotion, bears prowl with steadfastness, and thoroughbred horses gallop with great speed. All the world's animals and insects know to show off their innate skills and abilities well.

"Performing" must be conducted appropriately so as to be genuine and proper. We should never be pretentious and manipulative in what we do, especially within an organization. If we try to stand out above others and ignore team spirit, we will only earn the dislike of others. Proper performance can be a beautiful art, and a show of our abilities. Whatever our special skills and talents may be, we should perform them well!

Think, Speak, Listen, Act

If we want to succeed in life, there are four words we need to pay attention to: think, speak, listen, and act.

People cannot be without ideas and cannot stop thinking. We think, "I want to be a good person, a rich person, a good son/daughter, or a good wife/husband." We think about owning a house and having good food and clothing. Some of us aspire to the ideals of being a leader, a virtuous individual, or an important person. Ideals are the causes of reality, and reality is the result of ideals. Without a cause, how can there be a result?

Thinking alone is not enough. We need to speak out and make our thoughts known. For instance, we may want to drink tea, eat, get a ride, study, or find a job. We have to tell people what we want or can do. Otherwise, they will have no idea. Babies cannot talk, so they cry when they want milk. Dogs wag their tails or bark to express themselves. If we are seeking the best care from our parents, support from our friends, love from our lovers, or attention from our bosses, we must speak out. Of course, we cannot just say anything; what we say should be well put, fair, and substantial.

In addition to speaking out, it is important to know how to listen. A young man wanted to learn public speaking. The tuition was $10 per hour for such a course. However, when he met his teacher the first time, he started to talk nonstop about how important it was to know how to speak well. After he finally finished talking, his teacher asked him for $20. The student asked, "Everyone else only pays $10. Why do I have to pay $20?" His teacher replied, "I only teach others how to speak, but for you, I also have to teach you how not to speak and how to listen. So your fee is double."

Knowing how to listen is the biggest lesson in life. We have to listen well, completely, and carefully. In addition, we must listen for the message in between the words and its moral implications. Parents often blame their children for not listening well. Teachers complain about young people refusing to listen because the latter often only hear twenty or thirty percent of what has been said. They easily get the opposite message, mistaking east for west. We should also be careful not to take anything out of context and not to misunderstand a kind intention. Not listening is bad, but hearing the wrong message is even worse. Therefore, it is most valuable if we can listen and understand a sentence thoroughly, and act on it as appropriate.

Some people tend to be arrogant. They are deluded in thinking, talk without really speaking, look without seeing, and hear without listening. Naturally, it is difficult for them to "act." When we see others doing well in everything they do, it may appear very easy. In reality, a person's success needs certain conditions. Boy and girl scouts do a good turn daily. Having the courage to do what is right is a good turn. Likewise, believing in the Buddha or paying respect to him is not as good as practicing the teachings of the Buddha. Giving others assistance and service is also doing a good turn.

Thinking well, knowing how to speak, listening attentively, and acting benevolently are the four qualities we should have in life, because they are critical for success!

Setting a Good Example

In education it is far better to teach by personal example than with empty words. If we ask others to be good, we must first set an example ourselves with our own actions. Benjamin Franklin once said, "A good example is the best instruction."

One day, while taking his students on an excursion, Wang Yangming, the Ming Dynasty philosopher who advocated that actions should be in accord with knowledge, came across two women quarreling on the side of the road. The first woman accused the second one of not having a conscience, and the second woman accused the first of not living by the law of nature. Upon hearing their heated words, Wang Yangming turned to his students and asked them to listen carefully to the teachings of the Way. The students were confused by their teacher's request, because they thought that the women were merely abusing each other verbally. Wang Yangming explained, "When they ask each other to have a conscience and live by the law of nature, they are engaged in idle arguments, but when we apply their demands to ourselves, we are learning about the Way as it should be." Thus, true education lies in setting high standards to follow.

When Ji Kang, a disciple of Confucius, sought the master's advice on the proper way of government, the master replied, "To govern properly is to be honest and virtuous, just, and unbiased." For our citizens to behave in the right way, our leaders must take the lead in setting good examples. On a battlefield, the commanding officer must station himself at the head of his troops in order to win. In a classroom, a teacher must practice what he/she teaches for the students to trust his/her words. Similarly, parents must set good examples in order to teach their children properly. If they were to stay out all night partying with friends, how could they impose a curfew on their children? If they take drugs themselves, how can they expect their children to say no to them?

The behavior of today's youth often follows the wrong track.

Although they must shoulder part of the blame, it is not all their fault. Parents must also take a good look at themselves for the causes of their children's wayward behavior. For example, parents tell their children to be honest, but they lie at will. They ask their children to do volunteer work and partake in community service, but they are selfish and stingy themselves. If the parents' actions do not match their words, how can they expect their children to listen and obey?

One day a student was caught stealing a pencil from another student. The teacher notified the boy's parents. When the parents picked up their son from school, they were furious, "What have you done? If you had wanted pencils, we could have gotten a bunch for you at work!" It is truly ironic to see parents teaching their children not to steal, yet at the same time, committing the same offense. Under such circumstances, it would be very difficult for any child to be an upstanding citizen when he/she grows up.

Nowadays, it is not uncommon to see corrupt politicians asking their constituents to be law-abiding citizens. There are selfish and conceited bureaucrats who ask society to practice propriety and virtue. It really begs the question when those who lack decency themselves are making demands of others to be decent.

After becoming the Enlightened One, the Buddha still took care of disciples who were sick and old. He would personally prepare their meals, mend their robes, and administer their medicines. The Buddha's actions are perfect examples of how one can help others with compassion and loving-kindness. Even at the age of eighty, the Buddha was still diligent in his daily routines, such as going into town for alms. By being mindful in his practice, the Buddha set an excellent example for his disciples to follow.

It is by setting a good example for those learning from or working for us that we can truly become teachers.

Self-Deprecation

People are usually averse to others speaking of their shortcomings. For instance, being too short or not handsome enough, having a poor voice or being inarticulate are weaknesses we do not want others to make fun of. In reality, nobody is perfect, so we should not be embarrassed about our vulnerabilities. If we have a sense of humor and joke about them, we can actually live a more carefree life.

In running for office, candidates often make fun of themselves while speaking about their election platform so that their audience will have a good laugh. There is nothing wrong with self-deprecation as it can attract more attention, help make a deeper impression, and may even win the respect of others.

Making fun of oneself can sometimes also help ease an embarrassing situation. Once Socrates' wife scolded him and then threw a basin of water at him in front of his friends. When everyone became very embarrassed, not knowing what to do or say, Socrates calmly said, "I know that after it thunders, it will certainly rain."

One time after Venerable Master Yuanying spoke the Dharma, the leading chanter was, according to Buddhist etiquette, supposed to say: "Strike the gong, and escort the Elder Monk to the dormitory." But because he was too nervous, he said instead, "Strike the Elder Monk and escort the gong to the dormitory." On hearing that, Venerable Yuanying replied as he was walking, "No need to strike me, I will leave." A few self-deprecating words resolved the embarrassment for the lead chanter. Yuanying was truly an elder monk of deep cultivation.

A young soldier was returning to the barracks after vacation and was carrying two ducks. He met his captain on the way who asked, "What are you carrying?" The soldier was already very nervous about seeing his commander, but it was even worse to be questioned. He stuttered, "Duck, I am carrying two captains." His captain replied, "I am very heavy, you can't possibly carry me."

Once, an air force lieutenant general was celebrating his birthday with his staff. During the party, an attendant serving the general was too nervous and spilled a whole glass of wine on the bald head of his superior officer. The entire party became silent waiting for the general to blow up. However, the general just said gently, "Do you think you can cure my baldness with this? If that works, I would've done it myself a long time ago."

People who know how to be self-deprecating are undoubtedly wise, cultivated, and sympathetic. If someone in a senior position can resolve unintentional offenses by his/her subordinates with self-deprecation, it is a form of compassion.

I Assumed

"I assumed" is a phrase used by many people to cover up mistakes or errors, such as paying an exorbitant price for a fake antique. It is used when making an assumption far from the truth, such as mistaking an innocent bystander for a thief, shirking responsibility, or by claiming innocence in a crime, saying that you did not know a sharp knife or a deadly poison could kill. It is an attempt to place the blame elsewhere, which is of serious consequence and can lead to disastrous results. There are simply too many "I assumed" excuses in this world: I assumed the storm would not come; I assumed it would not flood; I assumed he could swim; and I assumed it would not hurt. No matter what the outcome might be, the expression is just a way for the responsible party to say, "I cannot be held accountable for what happened!"

"I assumed" can be perceived as stubbornness, an attempt to make excuses, such as letting a common cold turn into something far more serious because "I thought I would never become so ill." Since any phrase can be taken either positively or negatively, "I assumed" can be a joke or a knife through a person's heart. If our homes are robbed at night, we will most likely blame each other for being careless. Everybody's favorite excuse in such a situation is "I assumed you had already checked all the doors and windows." Similarly, when breakfast is not ready in the morning, we blame everyone else in the house for not getting up early enough. Amidst echoes of "I assumed," the seeds of discord are sown with subtle accusations.

Despite its many negative effects, "I assumed" can also be very positive, such as cleaning the house and cooking dinner because "I assumed" everyone would come home late from work. I kept an eye on my neighbor's house because "I assumed" they were out of town. I made an extra dish because "I assumed" your parents were coming for a visit. I lent you some reference books because "I assumed" you might need them for your test. I fixed the roof because "I assumed" the storm might come soon. I prepared extra food for the holiday dinner because "I assumed" our friends might want to eat with us.

We should always base our judgments on real substance and scientific deduction instead of assumptions and expectations if we do not want unpleasant surprises and disappointments. When the Japanese army invaded China in 1937, they believed that they could sweep unimpeded across the country in three months. However, history proved them wrong. After the 9/11 terrorist attacks on the United States, President Bush promised the American people that he would defeat the Taliban within forty-eight hours of the first strike and capture Osama bin Laden thereafter. As of today, bin Laden's whereabouts remain a mystery.

Most of the time, "I assumed" are just words of conjecture that are meaningless and irresponsible. In many cases, they have led to family quarrels and workplace animosity. Although at times it may be appropriate to say, "I assumed," it can be very damaging when it is taken out of context or spoken improperly. Therefore, it is imperative for us to think before we utter those two little words.

The Thought Process

Since the human mind is much more evolved than that of an animal's, a human being has the ability to think rationally and coherently. A person can use his or her mind to improve the world and determine his/her own future. Whether a person is engaged in political activities, business ventures, educational issues, or scientific research, his/her mind must be flexible and resourceful. For example, a person must have more than one course of action in planning a career. A negotiator must have more than one strategy in negotiating a deal. An employer must have more than one candidate in mind when hiring for a position. A student must have more than one choice in applying for college. Therefore, how can the thought process of an intelligent human being lack resourcefulness when even a wily rabbit has three burrows in which to hide itself?

Having a first, second, and third course of action for addressing any problem gives us room to adjust. It provides us with different choices, a clearer sense of priorities, and gives us greater convenience and expediency. In a competition, if we win first place, we will no doubt feel thrilled and satisfied. However, if we come in second or third, we should not be too disappointed because we still have the opportunity to be on the podium to receive a prize. No matter what, if we handle our affairs resourcefully and keep our priorities straight, we will have the joy and experience of wearing a medal of some kind around our necks.

Once upon a time, there was an avid horse rider who would always lose when racing others. One day, out of frustration, he consulted a well-known military strategist to get advice on how to win. The strategist advised him to race his slowest horse against his opponent's fastest horse, his fastest horse against the opponent's mediocre horse, and his mediocre horse against the opponent's slowest horse. In that way, he would always win two out of three races. Therefore, in competition, if we are to win, we must use our heads. Only through resourceful thinking can we translate defeat into victory.

If we are to seek perfection and satisfaction in this world, we must not be single-minded. We must have a first, a second, and a third plan of action. Although many things in the physical world require simplicity, such as having one country, one family or one spouse, the rule of singularity does not apply to the human thought process. With regard to mental activity, single-mindedness is unacceptable. The human mind must be capable of more than one level of thinking. It must make room for a first, second, and third course of action if it is to acquire more depth, insight, and progress.

Life Planning

"Life planning" is a popular concept in today's world. People make long-term plans for money, careers, and raising a family. Some people even take the steps to plan for memorializing their ancestors, the future lives of their children and grandchildren, or their long-term contributions to society. Of course, there are also people who only plan for the month ahead based on their monthly wages, or even day to day when they are paid daily. Other than planning three meals a day, some people do not have enough resources to plan for anything else. Others can only plan their own existence and not anyone else's. It is not easy to plan for the future completely in this world of ours.

Confucius summarized his life in this way: "By thirty I was established; by forty I was without doubt; by fifty I knew my mission in life; by sixty I was undisturbed by anything I heard; and by seventy I could follow my wishes without transgressing the Way." This is indeed life planning!

In traditional Indian culture, life is planned as follows: self-study until twenty, serve others until forty, teach until sixty, and travel until eighty. There are scholars in the past who planned life in the following manner: the thirties devoted to literature, the fifties to philosophy, and the seventies to history. People today, however, generally plan life according to their professions and develop careers within those boundaries.

In Buddhism, the practices of "compassion and wisdom," "merit and wisdom," "understanding and cultivation," and "compassion, loving-kindness, generosity, and joy" also form the basis for life planning. People can plan their lives based on their respective qualities. For instance, those who are articulate can lecture and teach; those who are good writers can get involved in publishing; those who are intellectual can conduct research; and those who are generous can perform charity work.

In reality, there can be no absolute plan for life because we all have different causes and conditions, and we sometimes face circumstances beyond our control. Therefore, the best plan is actually to manage ourselves well by pursuing a life of enlightenment, self-help, and helping others. In life, we should have love and sentiments that are untainted by selfishness, money that is spent for worthy purposes, and high morals in dealing with situations. Our mission should be to transform social mores for the better so that our lives can become truly meaningful and worthwhile. That is the best planning for life.

Quality of Life

Nowadays, people are very particular about the quality of life. What constitutes quality of life? It is not about eating sumptuous meals, driving luxury cars, hosting parties, or being social. Nor is it about working day and night without a moment of relaxation or being in meetings all day and leaving no time for leisurely activities.

Quality of life refers to leading a disciplined life and having a clean environment, a quiet home, a safe neighborhood, and three regular meals. It is having a peaceful household, an orderly society, a normal routine where there is a good balance of work and play, and a fixed schedule of daily activities. It is having a strong belief in the right faith that promotes benevolent deeds and discourages the pursuit of fame and fortune. It is serving society and taking time to read newspapers or a good book. It is appreciating arts and music and being in touch with the world of culture and education. It is making time for the family daily, relatives and friends weekly, and some cultural or educational activities monthly.

If we are to have quality in our lives, we need music in our homes more than an air-conditioner, a shelf full of books more than a cellar full of wine, and a healthy family relationship more than expensive furniture. We should not equate quality of life with having a grand home, a big garden, a fleet of cars, or a trendy wardrobe. What we really need to emphasize in assessing quality of life is a family's outlook on morality and proper behavior, the passing down of a philanthropic tradition, excellence in both morals and academics, helping and forgiving others, and offering laughter and earnest praise.

On entering the home of a rich and powerful family, we may be greeted with a chilly air of haughtiness, a team of servants, and a collection of expensive artifacts. What we see and feel is nothing but luxury and extravagance. However, true quality should be found in honesty, benevolence, righteousness, composure, and gentleness. A reporter once visited the home of Mei Lanfang, the renowned Chinese opera singer, for an interview. During their conversation, which lasted several hours, they were rarely interrupted. The house was peaceful and harmonious, and even the maids and servants were serene and unhurried in their steps. The reporter was very impressed with the actor's high quality of life. Mencius' mother moved several times in search of a good learning environment for her child because she had a high regard for the quality of life. The mother of Yue Fei, a loyal general in Song Dynasty, taught her son loyalty because she wanted him to have a life of high spiritual quality.

Life should be about quality and not quantity. To have quality in life, our civic leaders should lead by example so people can follow the ways of simplicity and courtesy. Hosts should keep an orderly household and be courteous to guests. Businesses and industries should treat each other and the public with respect and honesty. Students should be respectful in everything they do, government employees should put service first, and public enterprises ought to be thoughtful and considerate. If everyone can act accordingly, from top down and vice versa, everybody will be able to lead a life that is praiseworthy.

What we call the Pure Land of Ultimate Bliss in Buddhism really represents the quality of life to which all sentient beings aspire. Similarly, the Eastern World of Pure Crystal Radiance offers a world of order and prosperity all sentient beings admire. Therefore, quality of life is something all of us should pursue vigorously in order for it to be fully realized in our world.

The Tracks of Life

In life, we race on many tracks. In terms of professions, there are jobs in academia, agriculture, manufacturing, business, etc., from which to choose. In our studies, we can specialize in literature, history, arts, science, philosophy, computer science, or something else. Which track do we want to get on?

Some people like to tread on only one track and finish life as such. There are others who keep changing tracks. They work for a few different companies within one year and may end up going nowhere. However, some of them do succeed in finding their real interests by changing to a new track. Some people may be talented and capable, but they either indulge in the pursuit of sensual pleasures or slack off doing nothing. They fail to get on the right track in life. There are others who cannot find their track. They face too many obstacles or experience a tough time. Then there are those who fail to see clearly, imagining that "the grass is always greener on the other side."

When airplanes get on the wrong runway or cars drive down the wrong lane into oncoming traffic, there is the danger of a collision. The damage can often be unthinkable. In looking for the right tracks in life, we should consider the ones that keep us safe with no danger of derailment. We need the guidance of benevolent teachers to stay on track in life, like airplanes needing the direction of the control tower. Loyalty, integrity, righteousness, justice, trust, diligence, and compassion are all the right tracks in life. The Noble Eightfold Path in Buddhism is the track leading to a bright future. These should be our tracks for life.

The many tracks of life—love, family, society, economics, politics, and career—regardless of which one we are on, are all related somehow. What is important is not derailing from whatever track we are on, and making sure that it is safe. Such a track is truly the right one for us. But sometimes it is not just about us racing forward on the same track. It is more important that we treat one another with courtesy by giving others room, and yielding in the same manner we would when driving.

"Where there is a will, there is a way." Sometimes we need to find and open up our own path. Many Chinese want to create a new world for themselves overseas. So we see many people of Chinese descent fighting their way to many regions of the world, charging forward on a foreign track and gaining success. There are others who prefer to live the life of a recluse staying out of the limelight. They do not seek fame and fortune but instead study and write, finding their own track in life.

Historical figures have shown us their tracks: poet Tao Yuanming was on that of a hermit; General Yue Fei was on one of loyalty; Sir Thomas More was on one of integrity; Albert Einstein was on the track of science; and Babe Ruth on that of baseball. People need to tread on their own tracks. However, it is also best when we can walk on the path of ethics and morals, a path that benefits humanity. It is the great path the entire world should be paving for all to tread.

To Save and Prepare

Bees gather nectar for the winter, and ants collect food for storage. Squirrels store nuts for times when food is hard to find. These are examples from nature of saving for a rainy day, a good habit we all should adopt. We should have flashlights ready for the night and umbrellas for the rain, and we, too, should store up some food for a possible calamity if we understand the meaning of being prepared.

Humankind is indeed good at saving up and being prepared. To save does not mean to be greedy. Some people may already have a million dollars in assets, but they may wish for ten. When they have ten million, they may wish for even more. There are those who are multi-millionaires, but they will not give a penny to help others. This is stinginess and greed. These people have become enslaved by money. They may enjoy great wealth, but hoarding it in this manner is meaningless.

The true meaning of saving up and being prepared is to develop an awareness of changing conditions, to be on guard, and to plan ahead. For instance, we should check our windows and doors at night to prevent break-ins. During the day, we should have food and beverages ready for visitors. At work, we should have information and materials ready in case we need them. Our car should be equipped with a spare tire for an emergency. The belief in saving up for a rainy day and being prepared for emergencies is important to have in life. In reality, we should not only save up money and food, we should also save up human resources, good connections, and merits, which we can use for the long days ahead.

As the saying goes, "Being prepared frees us from trouble, and endless trouble springs from being unprepared." We should always be on guard for disasters and emergencies in order to spare ourselves from unnecessary suffering. For example, we should not cut down trees indiscriminately, but instead we should plant more trees. That is the way to prevent environmental problems, as trees help prevent soil erosion, create oxygen, provide shade, and make our world beautiful. We should work on preventing erosion on hillsides during the dry season so that when the rain comes, landslides can be prevented.

People live better material lives as their savings in the bank increase. However, in life, we should not only care for saving money and material resources. We should also save up on morals, compassion, integrity, and knowledge. These are the positive causes and conditions for establishing ourselves and dealing with the world. They are resources that can serve us in endless ways.

The nations of the world rank the power of a country by the strength of its defense and the size of its monetary reserves and economy. Some countries are endowed with a wealth of resources, but most people just focus on saving money rather than morals, and amassing short-term uses instead of long-term strengths. They only save up results instead of the conditions that produce them, material things instead of the knowledge that underlies them, and reputations instead of the trust that supports them. They do not have a sense of awareness in guarding against the pollution of their minds, the problems in their lives, and the unwholesome causes and conditions of their environment. So when a disaster takes place and they are not prepared, they can find themselves in real danger, just as a dyke can collapse due to a tiny crack. Therefore, how can a life without saving or preparedness be free from danger?

One's Footing in Life

In the course of life, it is important for us to find our footing. Where is our footing? We can find our footing in our home because it is a place of comfort after a long day of work; in our friends because they provide us with knowledge and support; and in our work because it can offer us a sense of honor and achievement.

If we want to establish ourselves in this world and get along with others in society, we must first find our own footing. Otherwise, we may infringe on others, taking advantage and using them as our "footing." We see two countries go to war with each other because one of them wants to occupy the other's territory and turn it into its own footing. We see two parties who are unable to cooperate with one another, because they are unwilling to share the same footing.

When we find our footing in our family or an organization, we will cherish its members. If a group of people agree to meet at a specific time and place, they will not break their promises no matter how long the separation, because in keeping to their arrangements they share a common footing.

When an airplane flies across the sky, its flight path is its footing as it must take off and land on an assigned runway to avoid collisions. When a train leaves the terminal, it will make a number of stops before it arrives at its final destination. No matter how far the train travels, every scheduled station on its route is part of its footing. Similarly, when a ship sets sail on the ocean, each port of call is a part of its footing.

If a tree is to grow tall and strong, it must have deep roots as its footing. If a house is to be built properly, it must have a stable foundation as its footing. The Greek mathematician Archimedes once claimed that with the right footing, even the Earth can be moved. In terms of the theory of leverage, this hypothesis is entirely accurate.

So, where can we find our footing in life? We should find our footing by respecting our parents, being diligent and responsible, cultivating ourselves, nourishing our true nature, enduring hardships, and working hard. We should ground ourselves by making sacrifices and contributions, having respect and tolerance for others, being compassionate, and practicing joy and equanimity for the benefit of others. Most importantly of all, if we are to live our lives in accordance with the law and embark on the right path, we should find our footing in right views, right understanding, and right discipline.

Marriage

Most people understand marriage as a man and a woman living together as spouses. In reality, marriage is not just a matter of compatibility between a man and a woman. It also involves family backgrounds in "a match of comparable households." Their finances and education should be of a similar level. However, even when all qualities appear to be well-matched, if the values and views of the couple are different, it is difficult for the marriage to last.

Once, there was a young couple engaged to be married. The young man's family often held parties and gatherings for the entire clan. Whenever the young woman was invited over for these dinner parties, she would see the married sisters of her fiancé showing off their riches and accomplishments to each other. The unpretentious young woman found the etiquette and manners at these dinners more than a little overwhelming. In the end, she broke up with her fiancé, whom everyone else considered to be her perfect match.

Even after a couple is married, their life together cannot be sustained merely by a marriage certificate. They need to share similar interests, hobbies, social lives, and conversational interests in order to link their hearts together. There was a wife who loved to listen to cello music before she married. She pleaded with her husband to go with her to cello performances, but he always refused using different excuses. Finally, without telling him, she bought two tickets for a concert, leaving him no choice but to go with her. However, when the concert started and before the first piece was even finished, her husband fell asleep, snoring loudly in harmony with the cello on stage. No matter how she pushed, pinched or kicked him, he continued to sleep. She felt so lonely watching him sleep that she shed bitter tears.

Sometimes a marriage is threatened when a couple has different views on how to raise their children. There was once a professor who fought with his wife over how to educate their children. She was so angry that she wrote a letter to the Defense Department saying that he spied for the enemy and went to their secret meetings. As a result, he was jailed for more than ten years.

Socrates once joked, "Because I married a shrewd woman, I became a philosopher." However, not everyone is as cultivated as he was. In real life, many people leave home and travel to faraway places because of a bad marriage. Some study abroad or join the armed forces to get away from spouses whom they have found to be intolerable.

Some couples date for years before they marry, but within a few, short months of marriage, they want to part ways because they discover they have different interests, living habits, and values. When shopping, they may have different preferences for colors and designs. They may not agree on the way furniture in their house is arranged, and even fight over how to squeeze a tube of toothpaste. Such is an illustration of the saying, "They marry because of misunderstanding and separate because of understanding."

In the past, many people entered into marriages that were arranged by parents and matchmakers and managed to make the marriages last a lifetime. They could do so because of mutual respect and tolerance. So arranged marriages were not a problem for them.

Some people are too strong-headed. They want everything to go their way and become very disappointed when their wishes are not fulfilled. Because of their attachments, they fail to seek commonality with others and do not tolerate different opinions or ways. With such a personality, they will find it difficult to make friends, marry, and get along with others. Even if they become monastics in a religious group, they still will not be able to cope well within the organization because of their incompatibility with others.

If Christopher Columbus had had a suspicious wife who continually asked questions–Where are you going, who are you going with, what do you want to do, why did that woman (the Spanish queen) give you three ships?–how would it have been possible for him to reach the Americas? The prime conditions for a happy marriage are for a couple to have mutual trust, help, support, and forgiveness in order to make up for one another's shortcomings and to create a beautiful future for themselves.

One's Family

The people closest to us in the world are our family members. It is said, "Those not of the same family will not enter the same door." When we spend a long enough time with our family, we end up sharing each other's views, spirit, and habits. However, even in the same family, there are times when different viewpoints surface and arguments can ensue. Because of work or study, members of a family have disparate schedules, but since they are of the same family, they should be understanding and tolerant of one another.

In the same family, some people like music and others literature, sports, travel, or meditation. Even when their interests and personalities vary, they should admire each other's character and respect one another's existence. Because of their gratitude for parental nurturing and natural bonding with their siblings, family members are more willing to go through thick and thin together. Though there may be a big argument one day, everything will usually be fine the next.

Therefore, the home should be a nest of peace and harmony, a safe harbor in life. Family members are always our support, and the home is the pit stop that never closes for replenishment. Those traveling abroad for some time will want to come home when they can to share their feelings with family members. They can talk about their successes and setbacks and the gains and losses they have realized, because their family will not betray them. Family is a recycling center that will not reject anything from its members.

However, even when all family members share the same food and shelter, they can still have different personalities. They may be loyal, treacherous, wise, or foolish. Some children enhance the family morale, bringing glory to its members. But there are those who squander the family fortune and estate. Being part of the same family, members should always support each other with encouragement and emphasize the importance of contributing to the family peacefully in order to preserve its lineage over time.

A family usually consists of blood relations. But people who are not related to one another by blood can also become a family. For instance, practitioners living and working in a temple come from all backgrounds, and they are not related. However, because of their faith and Dharma lineage, they are as close as family. There are people who consider each other family for other reasons. Examples of such are foster or adopted children and "sworn" brothers and sisters. People with different family names can also be part of one family. Christians belonging to the same order often address one another as brothers and sisters, and in Buddhism, whether they are monastics or laity, practitioners refer to each other as "dharma brothers and sisters." It means they consider one another family members.

Family is not limited to the same surname or origin, and neither is it confined within the same house. It can be expanded to "universal brotherhood within the four oceans." The world today is a global village, and "the corner of heaven is as close as next door." When we consider all nations and races in the world as our family and siblings, are we not further enhancing global harmony?

Family is the key unit to any human organization. When we start from this key unit and expand the love and closeness of a family to all of humanity, the notion of family will certainly become much more meaningful.

Aspects of Human Sentiment

Some societies of the world place much emphasis on human sentiment, while others place theirs on either the rule of law, or customs and principles. The Chinese culture has been heavily based on human sentiment. There is even a saying, "If one is polished in dealing with human relationships, one is proficient in literary undertakings." From a young age, we are taught by our parents about the civilities of human relationships. As we mature in life, if we fail to fully appreciate and apply the finer points of human sentiment, our associates and society will find us to be unacceptable members of the community.

In terms of receiving favors or gifts, or treating others and returning favors, we often feel we do not owe others anything. If we are indebted to someone, we cannot find peace and may even have trouble sleeping at night because of our debt of gratitude. There are of course people who ignore human relationships and fail to act with civility toward others. They carry on, handling their affairs and dealing with others in their own stubborn way, prompting people to criticize their unrefined conduct.

According to tradition, Chinese people have long recognized the importance of both fraternal and maternal relatives. When we make connections with our cousins near and far, we rely on the bonds of human sentiment. In building such relationships and establishing connections, we sometimes try to take the "backdoor," pulling strings based on family ties. When needed, we often attempt to get favors from our relations, whether they are from the same town, school, political party, or profession. If none of them is useful to us in any meaningful way, we try to make use of their connections with others. Therefore, some people claim, "Everything is all right if there is a connection. Otherwise, all matters would be of concern." Such is the importance placed on the bonds of human sentiment.

In traditional communities, such emphasis can be greater

because "even when people are not closely related to each other, they are all close to the land." In other words, they make close connections based on communities, political parties, and schools they have in common. There is the saying, "When one is within a community, one cannot act according to one's will." Because human relationships are especially difficult and important to maintain in any community, one must be able to be flexible and make compromises.

The easiest mistake we can make regarding human relationships is not being thorough or acting in a way that is contrary to our feelings. Yet often it is difficult for us to know for certain whether or not our feelings for others are genuine. Therefore, people sometimes bemoan, "Sentiments are like flowing water, they are as thin as a sheet of paper, and they are cold like frost. When people are around, there are sentiments. Otherwise, all is empty."

In asking for help, we often rely on relationships, status, and past connections. In reality, it is hard to always measure the depth and weight of what we feel inside. For this reason, besides relying on connections and human relationships, we should not ignore good principles and the rule of law. It is actually much easier to set standards based on these than on human sentiment alone.

Buddhism advocates: "Rely on the Dharma and not on people." That means we should abide by reasoning and the truth but not by our sentiments. Since human relationships change all the time, it is fairer and more reliable to rely on reasoning. For societies that emphasize human sentiments, if they can learn to rely more on sound principles and the rule of law, then their standards for conduct can reach a higher level.

The Treasure of a Great Friendship

In this world, it is easy for us to know a person by his/her face, but it is very difficult for us to read his/her mind. Therefore, the meeting of minds is the true essence of a great friendship. However, it is not easy to know what is on the mind of another person, because just as no two faces are similar, no two minds are the same.

Therefore, recognizing people, and understanding matters and reasons in life are not as difficult as intimately knowing a person's mind. This is why when we lose a close friend who understands our ambitions and outlook on life, we will mourn his/her loss.

During the Epoch of the Three Kingdoms, Zhuge Liang and Zhou Yu together conspired to win the Battle of Red Cliff over the Yangzi River. They used every means at their disposal to defeat the enemy. However, victory was not won until they surprised the enemy by setting fire to their ships. They each devised their respective strategies by writing what was on their minds in the middle of their palms. When it became apparent that they had the same strategy in mind, both men were taken aback by each other's wisdom and astonished at their ability to read the other's mind.

In battle we must know our troops well; in politics we must really know the affairs of government; and in business we must know financial matters like the back of our hands. The same goes for the practitioners of Chan, who must not only know their minds well but also be of one mind with the truth.

"To know" is a kind of relationship and understanding. It is like fathers knowing their sons best and history knowing the truth best. Today's intellectuals all wish to become a part of society's mainstream. However, humanity is not about individual knowledge. It consists of the relations of interdependency and the recognition of causes and conditions. We must understand that knowing others well is crucial because nothing in this world can exist in and of itself. Everything is the product of mutual causation. Once we know the importance of dependent origination, we will understand the nature of impermanence in formation, abidance, decay and emptiness, such as in birth, old age, illness, and death. In knowing all these, we can realize the truth.

  Is it possible for us to know what is on the mind of another person? Han Xin, a famous general who helped found the Western Han Dynasty, had the morale of his troops on his mind. For Tang Emperor Taizong, who laid the groundwork for later prosperity during his reign, it was the welfare of his subjects. Meng Jiangnu, whose bitter cry over her husband's death at the Great Wall, had the loving memory of her husband on her mind. Parents always have the whereabouts of their wandering children on their minds. Confucius was mindful of the virtues of benevolence and righteousness. Zhuangzi only thought of wisdom. And the Buddha had the whole universe and every sentient being on his mind.

  "Close to the mountains, we know the sounds of birds. Beside a river, we know the nature of fish." When we know the nature of birds, they will fly toward us. When we know the nature of animals, they can be our friends. As humans, we have the ability to know everything about heaven, earth, the universe, and people of all ethnicities. It is like a carpenter who loves wood because he is familiar with all its characteristics, or a gardener who adores flowers because he knows them well. If we are able to know the world and the international community, how can we not love them as we love our own country?

  History is full of examples of those who were willing to sacrifice their lives for the sake of close friends. They were willing to do anything for those who could share their thoughts and feelings. Therefore, in making friends, we must treasure the value of getting to know one another well.

The Value of Good Neighbors

There is a popular Chinese saying, "Distant relatives are not as good as neighbors." Neighbors can offer a helping hand right away in times of emergency. Our children play with them, and homemakers talk to them about daily happenings and experiences. Together, neighbors can volunteer to keep an eye on the neighborhood against possible crimes. They are the ones we often show our creations to in what we do. Poet Tao Yuanming once wrote, "Neighbors often drop by, and we talk at length about the old days. Admiring special writings together, we analyze and discuss any point we have doubts about."

When we leave home, neighbors help watch our houses, babysit, look after our elders, care for the sick, feed our pets, and pick up the mail. When we have to move, they help clean and pack. Should there be a wedding or a funeral, neighbors show their support by assisting in the preparations. When something is broken, a handy neighbor can repair it. They help shop for groceries, and can also share a meal or special snack with us. Such exchanges are aptly expressed by another poet, Du Fu, in his "Visiting Guest": "Living so far from town, the dishes are simple; since we are poor, there is only an old bottle of wine. When the neighboring man is invited over to have a drink, we call across the fence for a spare cup."

In today's society, a neighborhood block watch and crossing guards can be set up to improve security. When a crime takes place, neighbors can call the police for assistance and help track down the culprit. There are two other major benefits of good neighbors. One is to provide mutual support because in providing others service, we can receive it in return. Secondly, we can learn from at least one of our neighbors. When we select someone benevolent to be with, we can enhance our knowledge and understanding of things. There is the example of Mencius' mother, who moved three times in order to find a good neighborhood so her son could learn well. Tao Yuanming wrote, "I wanted to live in the south village, not because the house was especially auspicious. I heard there were people with pure hearts in the area, people with whom I would be happy to enjoy the mornings and sunsets."

Confucius said, "We will not be alone if we are virtuous; the virtuous will always have neighbors." Besides choosing people with high morals as neighbors, the ancients would even spend money to "buy" them. During the Southern Liang Dynasty, a man called Song Jiya bought a very expensive house next to the renowned Lu Sengshen in order to be his neighbor. When Lu asked him how much he paid for the house, Song replied, "One million for the house, ten million for the neighbor."

Of course, there are also bad neighbors who have no regard for others. They may be undesirable characters who steal and resort to violence. They might be noisy late at night, dump garbage everywhere, use coarse language, pry into other people's business, and not clean up after their pets. During the mid-18th century, Russia was an aggressive neighbor that encroached on China's borders. Nowadays, there are many "neighbors" living in the same apartment building who never even say a word to each other.

When we socialize with good neighbors, we can learn from them and aspire to be as good as they are in morals and etiquette. On the other hand, if we fall in with bad neighbors we will be like "Orchids changing and losing their fragrance, and fragrant herbs turning into couch grass." Therefore, choosing a good neighbor is a major lesson in life. And we should also ask ourselves, are we good or bad neighbors?

The Ways of Home Life

Our home life, particularly during the early years, can have a profound effect on our future. What qualities constitute home life? They are being neighborly, living within our means, eating simply, being frugal, honoring our elders, loving our young, supporting our relatives, and being loyal and honorable. In developing a good home life, we should put others ahead of ourselves, be willing to accept disadvantages, sacrifice for the family's cause, win love with love, cultivate our minds and self-nature, establish a positive image, and be selfless, clean and tidy. The heads of a household should know how to cook well. And everyone should look after his/her own health because the whole family will be troubled and suffer if someone at home gets sick.

The home does not belong to one person, but to the whole family. Therefore, the sanctity of home life should be upheld by everyone in order to cultivate a happy household. Some men like to socialize outside the home all day and bring guests home at night, disrupting the normal life of the family. Consequently, problems will arise.

In the past, large families were quite common; however, nowadays, we mostly see small households. The traditional custom of Chinese people having three or even five generations all living under one roof is very rare these days. Some people do not want to go home, while others do not have one and become homeless. There are gregarious people who believe having more relatives at home means getting more work done quicker and easier. Others hold the view that too many people under the same roof are a waste of resources.

According to Chinese philosophy, one should manage one's family well before he/she can rule the country. In order for a family to be harmonious and filled with laughter, all its members must like one another. In deciding what sacrifices he had to make, a Chinese revolutionary thought of his own family and realized that others have families too, and as he loved his family, others also loved theirs. So he transformed his love for his family to love for his country. The new Republic of China was thus established.

There is a Chinese saying, "In loving a home, one should also love the crows around it." Besides loving our home, we should also care for the environment, neighbors, and community facilities related to our home. Our household should be bright and tidy. We should keep things simple and not stock up on unnecessary items as if we were living in a warehouse. It should be neat, clean, and pleasing to the eye. The home should maintain a shrine as its center for honoring ancestors and a Buddha or bodhisattva statue. We need not be superstitious about the "*feng shui*" of our home as long as it is well ventilated and bright. Having a good relationship with our neighbors and being supportive of each other are far more important.

Chinese people used to stress that "A charitable family always has much to celebrate." Nowadays, some people prefer to cultivate "a literate family." In doing so, every Chinese-speaking family can subscribe to the *Merit Times*, watch BLTV via satellite, join the Buddha's Light International Association, and pay a pilgrimage visit to Fo Guang Shan once a year. We should establish a Buddhist family and use Humanistic Buddhism as the common ideals of every member. These should be the ways of home life.

Nurturing the Body and Nature

Chinese scholars place a great deal of emphasis on nurturing both the body and our true nature. In nurturing our bodies, we may want to take vitamins, go on vacations, travel, engage in recreational activities, and eventually retire from our careers. We need to exercise, take up physical chores, watch our diet, and be one with nature.

Buddhism also speaks about nurturing the body. We should work and rest at the right times and control our diet. Our minds should have right views and right thoughts. We should reduce our cravings and carry less greed, anger, jealousy, and worry. We may also worship, meditate by sitting or walking, garden, or do other chores. These are all ways to nurture the body.

In addition to nurturing the body, we also need to nurture our minds and inner nature. Our nature is our foundation. Without nurturing the nature of wholesomeness and benevolence, we do not have a foundation. Confucianism teaches, "We should cultivate the spirit of wholesomeness." In Buddhism, we nurture our bodies and minds, but it is more important to realize our true nature.

Before we can realize our true nature, our minds need to be gentle, open, calm, and at peace. If the mind is closed, rigid, attached and deluded, it will be difficult for us to see our true nature. Our nature is like water, which should be clear as a mirror and pristine as the sky. However, the winds of ignorance, unwholesome karma, and stress can create rough waves. So in our cultivation, we need to direct the water of nature into the right channels in order to calm the waves and avert flooding.

We nurture our bodies for health reasons, and we nurture our nature to perfect our character. However, nurturing the body is not for the purpose of acquiring a strong physique so that we can overcome others in fights; likewise, nurturing our minds is not for the purpose of shutting ourselves off from the rest of the world and ignoring the welfare of our community. Those who do not cultivate vows, courage, strength, and reasoning when nurturing themselves will surely deviate from the right path.

Throughout history, many scholars have used education to nurture their bodies and their true nature, and many religious leaders have employed self-control and expanded their love for humanity to deepen the cultivation of their nature. Venerable Master Huiyuan remained on Mt. Lu for thirty years and was highly respected for his cultivation. Chan Patriarch Bodhidharma meditated for nine years facing the wall of a cave, solely for the purpose of nurturing his nature. Upon becoming monastics, disciples of the Buddha cultivated in the woods, by the water, or in caves. Chan practitioners in China, such as Chan Master Xuedou, remained for many years in a monastery with the hope of perfecting their cultivation so that when the time was ripe, these dragons of the Dharma emerged to benefit all sentient beings of heaven and earth.

In nurturing our bodies we maintain our form, and in nurturing our nature we perfect our minds. With both a healthy body and mind, we will have no fear of not living a good life.

Self-Nature

Mencius believed that human nature was benevolent, while Xunzi thought it was selfish. The *Treatise on the Awakening of Faith in Mahayana* [*Dasheng Qi Xin Lun*], on the other hand, suggests that human nature is both. It is the combination of what we are born with and what we learn in life. Our innate nature needs to be developed, and our acquired nature depends on learning. Human nature has the potential to attain Buddhahood; therefore, strengthening our realization of the Way is like galvanizing our nature.

The human eye can see, the ears can hear, the tongue can taste, the nose can breathe, and the body can feel. These are all innate capabilities born out of our nature. Zhuangzi said, "A horse's hooves can step on snow and frost, and its hair can insulate it against the cold and wind. It feeds on grass when hungry, and drinks water when thirsty. It leaps and jumps on its hind legs when excited. Such is the nature of a horse." All phenomena in the world have their nature: the sun, fire, water and wind each have their own powers. They all have the capacity to generate energy. The nature of music is harmony; for wind, it is movement; and for flowers, it is fragrance. Eagles glide and swoop, roosters crow at dawn, lizards lose their tails to save themselves, dogs watch their owners' homes, bees gather nectar, octopuses emit ink, and sunflowers bloom toward the sun. They all have their own nature.

The nature of an asura is belligerent, while that of a bodhisattva is compassionate. The stars, thunder, lightning, wind, clouds, and rain each have their own individual nature. As for people, children tend to cry a lot, and some women are fond of looking good. When we develop and bring into full play the human capacities of compassion, prajna-wisdom, and Buddha Nature, we are tapping into our natural potential. This potential can be developed, is equal for all, and innate in each of us. Whether we become wise or ignorant, noble or poor, deviant or ethical all depends on how we apply ourselves. There are people who possess intelligence, talent, and agility as part of their noble nature. Other people are so slow and lazy that they dull and obscure their nature.

Some men tend to be open, generous, and courageous. Having a heroic nature, they are willing to take risks. Some women have an eye for details and are gentle, delicate, and appreciative of beautiful things. No matter what the case might be, our nature needs to be excavated, just like gold and silver ore deep in the hills or the earth. If we do not do so, how will we obtain the precious treasure of our self-nature? How will we realize the potential of our nature? In the past, those with wisdom studied the writings of sages and valued the importance of benevolence, righteousness, humility, morals, justice, and peace. Nowadays, we need to build and encourage the nature of taking responsibility, and of being gregarious, just, and supportive of the truth.

The Buddha was enlightened to the truth after years of ascetic practice, and he proclaimed, "All sentient beings have Buddha Nature. It is only because of their delusions and attachments that they cannot be enlightened." Therefore, if we want to realize our self-nature and experience infinite life, we need to meld into the universe and live in coexistence with all things. Then our own nature and that of the Buddha will co-exist in equality.

Moral Life

If someone were to be compared to Emperor Nero, he/she would surely be upset. On the other hand, if the same person is described as a Thomas More, he/she may feel flattered. Nero was an emperor, and More was a prisoner of his king. Why would someone rather be compared to a prisoner than an emperor? The difference lies in their morals.

All humanity should cultivate morals. If there were no morals to guide us in society and our lives, what would the world be like? Everywhere we turn, there would be corrupt officials, dishonest businessmen, jealous and gossipy friends, and two-faced neighbors. The people around us would be full of ignorance, wrong views, attachments, fighting, corruption, and selfishness.

Confucianism defines morality as the right path to live. It is the most noble and supreme guideline in life. With morals in life, society and family can be harmonious, friends reliable, and people willing to help one another. Accordingly, teachers should take on the responsibility of instilling morals, teaching career ethics, and answering questions. Medical professionals should save lives and care for the sick as they would members of their own families. Workers should labor hard at manufacturing to serve their company. Businessmen should do business fairly. Soldiers should guard their country faithfully and courageously.

To cultivate morality in people, Confucianism teaches the Four Directions and Five Ethics. Buddhism teaches the Four Means of Embracing, Six *Paramitas*, Five Precepts, and Ten Wholesome Conducts. There are right views and right thoughts, generosity, forgiveness, humility, and gratitude to observe. We should also control our desires, work to benefit all sentient beings, have respect and tolerance for others, be gentle and kind, speak well, praise others, and be selfless and just. All of the above are ways to practice morality in life.

Buddhism and Confucianism both advocate morals. Confucius never spoke about strange powers or acts of God, and Buddhism does not espouse supernatural beliefs. Instead, both traditions emphasize the importance of compassion and morals. Humans are different from animals because we have a sense of morality.

Therefore, every person in the world should apply morals to his/her own life and be responsible for improving the community. Those with morals can often influence the people around them by the way they live. As the saying goes, "The wind of morals can surely subdue the grass of vice." Living according to one's morals is thus the best way to show others how they should live. In order to be successful in what we do in life, the most important step for us to take is to cultivate our morality.

Maintenance

Women maintain their figures with routine exercise and a balanced diet, and their complexion with good skin care. Our health also needs to be maintained by regular check-ups and other good living habits. In everyday life, everything related to our daily activities requires maintenance, including our cars, houses, and appliances. Even mountains and rivers have to be maintained to remain healthy and vital.

A house must be maintained from the inside out. We should clean and sweep our homes regularly. For instance, we must wash our kitchen floors, dust our living rooms, tidy our balconies, weed our gardens, and paint our walls from time to time. When building houses, after the cement is poured, we need to sprinkle water on the cement to help it set well. Starting from the foundation is basic maintenance. After a field is planted with rice seedlings, we have to keep up with irrigation, fertilizing, and weeding. Maintaining things well early on is important for later growth.

The maintenance unit of a state's public works repairs and maintains roads to ensure safety for pedestrians and motorists. Ships, boats, cars, trucks, and airplanes must be serviced regularly. For example, China Airlines has had more than its share of air crashes. There are many possible reasons for this, but if regular maintenance is kept up, many incidents can be avoided.

While machines, the environment, and everything else in the world all need to be maintained, the most important maintenance we have to perform is on our bodies and minds. Looking after the physical body is not only for good looks but also to reduce sickness. When we are ill, we have to expend valuable resources, and our families are burdened with worries and extra chores. So when one person is sick, the whole family cannot have peace. Therefore, those people who do not maintain their own health are in fact not taking good care of their family members. It is not enough that we only care for our bodies. Maintaining the mind is even more important. Trees, flowers, and plants are constantly attacked by cold, heat, bugs, ants, and pollution. Similarly, the mind is regularly invaded by the dangerous lures of wealth and fame, gossip, greed, anger, and jealousy.

How do we uphold the purity and ease of our minds? We need to pay attention to maintenance. We cannot allow our eyes, ears, nose, tongue, and body to become the master and "lead" our minds to commit various types of unwholesome karma. We have to protect the mind in order for it to be strong, self-determined, and reasonable. Our pure mind should lead our eyes, ears, nose, tongue, body, and thought so that we will not look upon what should not be seen, not listen to what should not be heard, not speak what should not be said, not indulge in what should not be eaten, not commit what should not be done, and not feel what should not be touched. It is like shoring up the foundation of a house so that there will be no fear of its collapse, or maintaining the roots of a tree so that it will not wither. When we maintain our minds well, allow it to be the master, and listen to its own words, the foundation will be correctly in place. We will no longer have fear of it acting up and playing tricks on us.

Self-Education

As individuals with self-esteem, we should not remain as children and students dependent on our parents and teachers. We should learn to educate ourselves instead of relying on others. We are the ones that know best our shortcomings, ignorance, and areas needing the most improvement. If we do not become our own teachers, who else can truly understand and help us acquire knowledge?

What do we need to teach ourselves? In order to live, we should at least learn how to cook our own meals. We should dress warmly when it is cold and lightly when the temperature goes up. We should be sensitive to the weather and care for our own health. If we are ignorant of the environment and our bodily functions, no one will be there to look after us.

Our shortcomings such as laziness, jealousy, delusions, inconsistencies, etc., may be masked by our good looks. While others may not see them clearly, no one knows the truth better than ourselves. Therefore, when only we, along with Heaven and Earth, are aware of our faults, we must be our own teachers in order to improve.

Buddhism teaches: "Relying on either self or the Dharma is in the end all about self-reliance." This is self-education. For example, we can educate ourselves by understanding the meaning of an analogy, inferring the rest from what is known, and knowing ten things by learning about one.

Self-education is also self-expectation and self-motivation. Throughout Chinese history, there have been many prominent examples. Famed political and military strategist Zhuge Liang became accomplished through self-education. Author of the Historical Records, Sima Qian, motivated himself by traveling widely and studying the archives. Renowned painter of nature, Qi Baishi, brought animals to life with his brush after carefully studying their habits. Master painter Zhang Daqian studiously embossed portraits from the Dunhuang Caves, becoming one of the most accomplished modern Chinese artists.

  Many famous inventors were self-educated. Great inventor Thomas Edison famously said, "Success comes from one percent of inspiration and ninety-nine percent of perspiration." The only formal education Edison ever received was a short time in elementary school. What contributed to his being a great inventor was solely the strength of his self-education. There were also some great inventors in Chinese history: Cai Lun developed the technology for making paper, Cang Jie for printing Chinese characters, and Wang Yunwu the indexing system for dictionaries. All of them succeeded through self-education.

  Self-education means studying on one's own and not depending on others. We should constantly reflect on ourselves, be self-aware, self-motivated, and self-enlightened. If we can find our true nature through self-reflection, then we will have succeeded in our self-education.

Governing the Mind

It is easier to govern a country than a family; easier to govern a family than another person; and easier to govern another person than one's own mind. There are ministers and generals who can govern a country very well, but they cannot get along with their spouses and children at home. Some people take good care of their family lives and manage people and matters outside the home with ease, but find it hard to manage their own minds. They cannot control their desire, anger, worries, and deviant views and are constantly troubled by emotions and cravings.

The mind is like tangled silk that needs sorting to be in good working order. It is like an ancient mirror that requires a good polishing in order to shine, or a wild horse that needs to be tamed. The mind is our master, leading the daily activities of our eyes, ears, nose, tongue, and body. Within our everyday activities, a single thought may ruin our lives or reputations, or help us gain success and fame. Buddhist sutras compare the ungoverned mind to the likes of thieves, vicious beasts, monkeys, and kings. Therefore, it is absolutely crucial to govern the mind! So what kind of power can we use to subdue the mind? The following are four suggestions that anyone can follow.

1. Know how to cultivate the mind. We repair furniture when it is broken, water pipes when they leak, and clothes when they are torn. If the mind has become smeared by greed, ignorance, and arrogance, how do we repair it? We need the instruments of compassion, joy, generosity, meditation, morals, and practice to treat it.

2. Know how to calm the mind. The mind is like a monkey or a horse. If we are not careful, it will commit all kinds of unwholesome deeds. Ming Dynasty scholar Wang Yangming said, "It is easy to capture a bandit in the mountains; it is difficult to catch the thief in the mind." Calming the mind is like

soldiers apprehending bandits or the police arresting thieves. Where are our soldiers and police? Right thinking is our soldier and right view is our police. We have to make good use of them in order to calm our minds.

3. Know how to use our minds. We are often manipulated by the mind but do not know how to use it properly. It is said that the mind labors for its physical form. It is often influenced by our desires and external circumstances. It is driven by sight, sound, smell, touch, and perception from outside. The greed, anger, and ignorance of the mind keeps pushing and working against us. So we must master our minds. With prajna-wisdom and clear understanding of sentiments and reasoning, we will understand how to use our minds.

4. Know how to understand the mind. Chan Buddhism speaks of "understanding the mind and seeing nature." This means that we need to have an awareness of our minds and be clear every moment. We should constantly watch the mind and not allow it to come and go as it pleases. We must not be enslaved by it. With right views and right thoughts to counter our roaming minds, we can contemplate and understand the mind and rest assured that we can accomplish anything.

Purifying the Mind

One of the many functions of the Buddha's teachings is to transform people's minds for the purpose of improving society. To this same end, some government officials have advocated a "Reformation of the Mind" movement. However, the idea of "reforming the mind" is somewhat inappropriate, because an undisturbed true mind does not naturally need reforming. What we simply need is to purify the mind of its defilements and worries.

Regardless of whether we are talking about reforming or purifying our minds, we must first have a set of principles as the foundation for our practice. Otherwise, we are wasting our time and effort. If we want to achieve pure mental clarity, we must be diligent in our cultivation, and not allow ourselves to be slaves of mere slogans and meaningless activities.

Why should the human mind be purified? It is contaminated by the "six dusts" of sight, sound, smell, taste, touch, and perception. It is covered with dust that needs constant cleaning and wiping. It is like a field of weeds that requires the use of a mower to clear it; a road obstructed by thorny branches that requires the use of shears to open it; or a rusty iron skillet that requires the use of a steel pad to restore its shine. Similarly, when the body is covered with dirt, we need soap and water to wash it clean.

What should we use to purify our minds of defilements? The teachings of the Buddha provide the best medicine for a mind that is spiritually ill and a society that is morally corrupt. Over the years, the Buddha's Light International Association has organized various activities for the sake of purifying the human mind and society. The "Campaign for Goodness" was held to promote kind words, good deeds, and good thoughts. The "Seven Precepts Movement" was launched to encourage people to say no to alcohol, tobacco, pornography, violence, lying, gambling, and stealing. The "National Campaign for Love and Compassion" was a nationwide event held in Taiwan for the promotion of loving-kindness and compassion. In actualizing the Buddha's teachings in the course of our practice, we are also awakened to the sufferings of others.

When the body is sick, we can seek medical help, but when the mind is defiled, we should look for guidance in the teachings of the Buddha. While physical ailments can be cured through medical science, spiritual malaise can only be treated through strong faith in the Triple Gems: The Buddha is the best doctor, the Dharma the best medicine, and the Sangha the best caregiver. Furthermore, Buddhist teachings on the Law of Cause and Effect remind us to exercise self-restraint and self-discipline. When we do this, we do not need to rely only on the restraints of civil laws to bind us. The Buddhist understanding of the intricate web of life, which is based on the Law of Dependent Origination, motivates us to take the initiative in protecting the environment and improving social customs. It purifies our minds and keeps them free from pollution.

At the same time, the Four Immeasurables of loving-kindness, compassion, joy and equanimity, the Six Perfections of giving, morality, patience, diligence, meditation and wisdom, and the Noble Eightfold Path are the best guidance for moral behavior. In addition, there are other methods of purification. For instance, forming good connections, understanding the mutual dependency and interconnectedness of people, spreading seeds of compassion, and cultivating the virtue of gratitude are all ways of purifying our minds through practice.

Stress and pressure, real or imagined, are a part of our lives because of what we see and hear everyday. The most expedient way for us to cleanse our minds of defilements is to use the water of compassion and wisdom. Only when our minds are free from dust can their full potential be realized without hindrance.

Losing Weight

"Gentlemen prefer dainty women." For a few thousand years, this verse from the Chinese classic *The Book of Odes* has had much influence on the traditional Chinese view that slenderness in women is beautiful. There is another famous anecdote that goes: "Emperor Cu loved women with slim waists, so concubines in the imperial palace would rather die from starvation than risk being neglected." As a result, women who wanted to be fashionable or to look beautiful in order to please their beloved all strove hard to lose weight. Some women's desire to look attractive for their loved ones is still relevant today.

People who are overweight can also be a sign of today's affluence in society. According to a recent medical survey, there are approximately one million people in Taiwan trying to lose weight. The cause of being overweight, excluding certain illnesses, is mostly overeating and lack of physical exertion. After people become overweight, they try various ways to lose weight, from drinking Slim Fast diet drinks to going on special diets or fasting. In the end, some go so far as to develop eating disorders such as anorexia. What suffering!

When a person becomes overweight, he/she needs to lose pounds. Similarly, when a country has spent beyond its budget, it needs to reduce its spending. When a company hires too many employees it has to downsize. For example, today there is too much tabloid news, so the media should trim back these publications.

When we are overloaded with worries and delusions, we have to let them go. When the burden of human relationships becomes too heavy, we need to lighten it. If our cravings have grown out of control, we need to curb them. As for clothing and daily necessities, we should keep them simple and be content with what we have. There is the saying: "The wise do not seek comfort in dwelling, nor fullness in food." *The Buddha's Bequeathed Teachings* [*Fo Yijiao Jing*] notes, "When eating, take food as medicine. Do not eat more or less according to likes or dislikes. Eating is only a means to nurture our bodies and to satisfy hunger and thirst, just like bees that extract nectar from flowers without ruining their color and fragrance."

Excessive weight increases the risk of diabetes, hypertension, and heart disease. It slows our physical movement and causes us to lose focus and spirit. That is why the Buddha once gave King Prasenajit of Sravasti a lesson on how to lose weight and stay fit.

Gaining weight is related to age, too. Upon reaching middle age, we tend to grow horizontally. A Chinese saying says, "A thousand taels of gold cannot buy slenderness in old age." In the past, appropriate weight gain was considered "good fortune." In Hawaii, when its native chief chose a wife, the standard was "the fatter, the prettier." In Japan, Sumo wrestlers are all very heavy. Hawaiian hula dancers should ideally be plump, and the plumper ones can actually make more money. Therefore, we should be heavy or slim according to our circumstances. However, it is important that we do so naturally and avoid falling into either extreme.

Being overweight is usually caused by consuming too many calories from fatty and sugary foods. While it is worrisome to be overweight, our bodies need certain fats to function well as they protect our organs and help us retain the correct body temperature. Fats are also one of three major nutrients that provide calories for the body. One gram of fat generates nine calories, which is twice as much as sugar and protein. If we eat more than our body needs, the calories will be stored under our skin, changing our figures as we put on weight. Therefore, people usually eat less in order to lose weight and look good.

Reducing food intake can help us lose weight. However, exercising is actually a better way to stay in shape. For instance, making pilgrimages, meditative walking, making prostrations, doing repentance service, and circumambulation are all good exercises for practitioners to maintain good health. By being optimistic and diligent and learning to let go, we can live with carefree and open minds. This way, we will stay healthy naturally.

The Meaning of Rest

Why is rest important? Because it enables us to move on further. According to Buddhist teachings, rest is one of the four kinds of motivational forces that help us in our practice. Rest is as important for people as fuel is for airplanes and ships. Without it we cannot function. Even troops need to retreat from the frontline to reorganize and rest sufficiently after each battle, so they can be ready to confront the enemy again.

An adequate amount of rest is vital. After an airplane has flown a long journey, even its metal gets tired. Everything, including the sun, the moon, and the stars, the mountains and oceans, and the great Earth, needs rest. Insects hibernate, roosters sleep early, industrious ants build nests for rest, and busy bees take a break after making honey. Governments and institutions are closed on weekends, so their officers and employees can take time off work. Rest is indeed crucial.

Unfortunately, some people abuse their right to rest. For example, some people use the need to rest as an excuse to sleep all day. Some hope every weekend is a long weekend, and others take long coffee breaks at work. These people rest in the morning, afternoon, and evening. They take off on all the mandatory holidays, and often even when there is no holiday. In finding every excuse to take off from work, life for them might as well be confined to a coffin where they can rest permanently!

Once, Aniruddha, one of the Buddha's disciples, dozed off when the Buddha was teaching. The Buddha chided him, "You foolish one who likes to sleep, you will be reborn as a shell creature and sleep for a thousand years, and never hear the Buddha's name." After that rebuke, Aniruddha was so ashamed of his bad habit that he practiced tirelessly without any rest until he eventually became blind. This time, the Buddha had a different lesson: "An appropriate amount of rest is also part of diligent practice!"

Sronakotivimsa, another enlightened disciple of the Buddha, was an accomplished zither player. The Buddha asked him, "What are the consequences when a string is either too tight or too loose?" Sronakotivimsa answered, "When the string is too loose, the instrument makes no sound. On the other hand, when the string is too tight, it snaps easily." The Buddha thus taught, "Cultivation is just like playing a string instrument. It should be neither too tight nor too loose. The middle path is the way to go."

Today's world is fast-paced. Unlike people in the past living in an agricultural society, people nowadays are so busy that they may not be able to share a meal with their family, get enough sleep, or even go home. Being busy is not a problem, but it is definitely not worthwhile if we risk our health in the process.

Rest is required for us to recharge ourselves. It provides an opportunity for us to relax in order to regain our energy and spirit. After proper rest, we should not hesitate to go back to where we left off. That is where the true meaning of rest lies!

Sculpting Ourselves

Parents usually want to shape their children into celebrities in some field or another when they grow up. Teachers want to mold their students to be even better than they are. Professionals in every field often groom the next generation, hoping that the new workers will actualize or perpetuate their ideals after they retire.

However, the most important thing in life is sculpting ourselves. Whether we want to become a politician or a millionaire, in sculpting ourselves, it is of prime importance for us to create an unblemished, righteous character. When we look at the work of sculptors today, there are some that look good on the outside while having very little substance within. Likewise, it seems that people do not care as much about beautifying their hearts as they do about their looks. They are willing to spend thousands of dollars to sculpt their bodies or to change their appearance through cosmetic surgery. This may make them appear more attractive and poised, but they lack inner beauty if their moral cultivation and wisdom are insufficient.

Sculpting ourselves is a life-long mission. It takes decades of work and endless patience because every bit counts, whether it is tangible or intangible. We need to be elegant not only externally in poise and etiquette but also internally in our morals and cultivation before we can project a noble character and the brilliance of humanity.

In sculpting themselves, some heroes of the past relied on benevolence and integrity to do so. Some women used chastity, some scholars wisdom, and some saints asceticism to shape themselves. Whatever method we use, sculpting ourselves is not for the purpose of winning the momentary admiration of others. It needs to be perfected over time. As the saying goes, "We can only know a person's heart over time and appreciate the strength of a horse over a long distance." Ultimately, we all have to pass the tempering of time in self-sculpting.

The British have traditionally wanted to sculpt themselves as ladies and gentlemen, the Americans as heroes, the Japanese as samurais, the Chinese as scholars, the French as romantics, and the Malaysians as hospitable people. Over the ages and kalpas, Buddhas and bodhisattvas all sculpted themselves as symbols of compassion and dignity.

According to a Buddhist sutra, "The mind is a painter that can create any matter." Our minds can sculpt us into a saint, a commoner, a ghost, an asura, a bodhisattva, a sravaka, a pratyeka-buddha, or a Buddha. People of wisdom, whatever life you wish to create for yourself can be achieved based on how you decide to sculpt yourself!

Maxims

Throughout the course of our lives, it is not unusual to be inspired by a phrase or an ideal that can later become a maxim on how we should treat others and handle ourselves. When we translate such an inspiration into a daily reminder for ourselves, the maxim can work like an earnest instruction from our parents and teachers.

What is a maxim? It is a brief statement of a principle, goal, or ideal. Although it is often engraved on a stone, a wooden tablet, or a piece of paper, it does not necessarily have to be so in order to serve its purpose. When General Yue Fei's mother wanted to encourage her son to be faithful in his duty as a soldier, she stitched the phrase "Serve Your Country with Unwavering Loyalty" on his back.

The most important thing about a maxim is that it needs to be permanently inscribed in our minds and not be forgotten over time. Throughout the ages, there have been different maxims for all kinds of people. While loyal subjects and pious sons have their principles, wise rulers and dutiful officials have their own ideals. Even scholars and entrepreneurs are not without goals. "To Obey Orders" is a soldier's motto. "To Be Honest with All Customers" is the standard for all shop owners. "To Teach without Discrimination" is a teacher's duty, and "To Have Humility, Propriety, Righteousness and Shame" is a student's obligation.

A maxim can apply to either a lifelong goal or a phase in a person's development. In either case, we need to imprint it in our minds and translate it into reality. Dr. Sun Yat-sen resolved "to achieve greatness instead of high-ranking positions" in his effort to democratize and modernize China. The Buddha vowed "to never rise from this seat of meditation until enlightenment has been attained." Master Yin Guang abided by the practice of "faithfully and earnestly reciting the Buddha's name" throughout his life. A Taiwanese taxi driver of forty years never received a traffic ticket because he was careful not to speed. His principle of putting safety ahead of everything else served him well throughout his long career.

Although there are many proverbs that can be used as maxims, we must take into consideration our own disposition when deciding which one is most suitable for us. An accomplished Japanese businessman has been able to rise above embarrassments and hardships to better himself, because he has lived by the maxim "to accept blame is the driving force behind all progress." A capable and reliable worker will never stray from the maxim "to always value dignity and punctuality over procrastination and tardiness, and to always uphold frankness and honesty over carelessness and reckless abandon."

A maxim is a self-prescribed goal, a self-determined direction for life. It is a constant reminder of what we should and should not do. For example, we should never be boastful of our own merits while disparaging the faults of other people. We should never obsess over what we have done for others and forget what others have done for us. A worldly reputation is not worthy of our envy, for benevolence is the virtue of the wise. In order to avoid libel and slander, we need to keep a low profile in all our deeds. Like the sages of old who assumed their own ignorance, we should always know our limitations; otherwise, we will overstep our boundaries. For this reason, Buddhist monastics are vigilant about the exhortation that "the wisdom of every being lies with you, and if you are not careful in guarding that wisdom, you will shoulder all the blame."

There are also maxims that caution us against impending disasters in our lives by reminding us of the relationship between causes and effects: "You can refuse to believe in anything but must have faith in the power of karmic retributions and rewards." Statements of admonition, such as "You would rather have all the world's people fail you than to fail any one of them," can have a positive impact on our lives and the ways we cultivate ourselves morally and spiritually. We should, therefore, have them imprinted in our minds as maxims of self-discipline.

To Rely on Ourselves

A practitioner was going with his friends on a long spiritual excursion. They feared that he did not have enough willpower to go through with it and cautioned, "This is a long trip, and there are five things we cannot help you with. They are walking, eating, sleeping, going to the bathroom, and carrying your luggage."

There are many things in life others cannot do for us. Others cannot take our place as we age, grow weak, or are sick and in pain. The Buddhist concept of karma reminds us that we reap everything that we sow. Only through our own efforts are we able to change our fate. Nobody else can learn for us, or develop our careers. Our actions, speech, and thoughts determine our future. We drink to quench our thirst, eat to ease our hunger, and in a democratic system, vote to exercise our rights.

There is a Chinese saying, "We rely on our parents while at home and on friends when we are away." Parents and friends are our conditions, but we are our own causes. We should realize that cause is the principal, and conditions are the external support. It is true that without the right conditions, a cause itself cannot come to fruition. For instance, a government needs the support of many capable administrators to prosper, but if its leader is lacking in virtue, no amount of talent and support can make the government run well.

Therefore, if we do not work hard, even when there are many positive external conditions, we will not succeed. If heaven were to rain diamonds and gold upon us, we will remain poor if we do not have the ability to pick them up. When we cannot personally accept a prize or trophy awarded us, we will not enjoy the honor and glory that comes with it. There are things in the world that can be replaced or altered. We call those conditions. But for everything else that cannot be replaced, we have to rely on ourselves. We can cool off under the shade of a large tree, and use a bridge to cross the river, but if we do not plant the tree or build the bridge, we cannot enjoy these conveniences.

All things rely on causes and conditions, but cause is more important. We are the "cause," and we can only rely on ourselves to reap the benefits of the right conditions. We need to cultivate our inborn kindness, good health, harmonious personal relationships, and hard work as our causes before we can gain the support of conditions.

A mother once told her son that there is no such thing as cause and effect in life, and if there were, she would be willing to bear them for him. One day, the boy cut his finger. As it bled, he screamed out in pain, "Mom, please hurt for me!"

There is no substitute for cause and effect. Sometimes we ask the Buddha and bodhisattvas for blessings to relieve our suffering. Yet even as we do so, we still need to rely on our own devotion and sincerity. Suppose we were caught in a flood, and a bodhisattva appeared in an unexpected form to rescue us. If we remain attached to our image of a bodhisattva and refuse to be rescued by anyone else, we will surely drown in the end.

If seeds are not sown, nothing will grow even with sufficient rain and fertilizer. Therefore, we can only rely on ourselves to sow good seeds to assure our own fortune and prosperity!

Develop Our Potential

A drunk was staggering along on his way home. As he passed by a cemetery, he fell into an open grave dug for the next day's burial. All night, he struggled to climb out, but his efforts were in vain. Suddenly, he heard something heavy fall in next to him. It was another drunk. He moved aside to watch how the other man would try to climb out so he could follow suit. However, the other man was as drunk as he was and could not get out after many attempts. Out of pity, the first drunk casually remarked, "Man, don't try anymore; you're not going to make it!" Not realizing there was someone else in the pit, the second drunk thought he had heard a ghost and was so startled that in one leap he landed outside the grave.

Everyone has inherent, limitless potential. In an emergency, even those who may seem weak in ordinary times can become very powerful. People who are usually inarticulate are able to debate with another point by point if they feel impassioned.

Human potential is like resources deep in the oceans or the mountains that must be excavated to be found. However, we often only use a very small fraction of our infinite potential. This is why there are many programs today to help develop our brainpower and intuition, as well as the potential of our children.

In order to develop our full potential, however, we need to recognize the intrinsic value of life. We all have unlimited capabilities. We should not underestimate ourselves by thinking: "How much talent can there possibly be within this physical body of five or six feet?" In reality, life is filled with endless potential. There are many examples of average citizens turning a seemingly hopeless situation around, or a foot soldier gaining great achievement. Therefore, we must have confidence in our ability to make major contributions to society and to accomplish great success in our careers.

We should also bravely face reality. Some people are frustrated by the fluctuations in human relationships and changes in society. They find it difficult to adjust because the reality simply seems too harsh. However, as long as we keep an open mind, develop our potential, and give ourselves a good evaluation, we can face reality with courage and perform with great success.

On attaining enlightenment, the Buddha said, "All sentient beings have the intrinsic nature to become a Buddha." If people can attain Buddhahood, is there anything in the world we cannot achieve? In truth, everyone has unlimited potential. Indulging ourselves in materialism and sentiment has obscured our true nature. We need to rid ourselves of the dust and defilements of our minds, and instead nurture our inherent true nature in order to fully develop our potential.

Self-Assurance

We should not be attached to our views, but we need to be self-assured. Some people may find it easy to be self-assured, but difficult to tolerate others' opinions at the same time. True self-assurance is the ability to encompass the views of others, instead of only being attached to our own. It is especially important for us to be self-assured about compassion, morality, charity, and other good deeds. Otherwise, we will give in to anger, self-indulgence, and harmful deeds.

African-Americans teach their children that black is the most beautiful color in the world and that they should be proud of their skin color and culture. That is an example of self-assurance. People who are constantly improving themselves will also gain self-confidence. On the contrary, those without confidence will not earn the confidence of others. When they are not sure about what they are doing, then naturally people around them will not trust them completely.

In Buddhism, when we speak of faith, it does not mean faith in the Buddha but faith in ourselves. We must know ourselves and have self-confidence. Sakyamuni Buddha was sure of himself and was able to overcome all obstacles in his cultivation. He finally attained enlightenment one night as he was gazing at the stars. The Sixth Patriarch Venerable Master Huineng had enough self-assurance that even though he was at one point assigned to husking rice in a mill, he was still able to see his self-nature and become the patriarch of his time. Therefore, on our journey in life, it is important that we are able to stand firm on our feet and accept any test. We must be responsible for what we think, say, and vow to do before we can win the approval of others.

There is a parable that illustrates self-assurance. Whenever wild geese flew over the nation of Yue, the people thought they were wild ducks, which were very abundant in the area. Whenever the geese crossed to the nation of Chu, where there were many swallows, the people there would mistake them for swallows.

As a pair of wild geese flew over these two nations, the female goose complained, "The people in these two nations are really confused. They mix us up with wild ducks and swallows!"

The male goose smiled and replied, "Don't blame them! It doesn't matter whether they see us as ducks or swallows. The fact is we are geese, and nothing is going to change that, right?"

We are ourselves. Even though there are trillions of people in this world, you are you and I am me. However, the sad thing is, most people neither have faith in themselves nor believe that their future is in their own hands. They turn to fortune-tellers and palm readers. They do not know that reading their hearts is far better than reading their palms. Our heart is our master because it is the origin of all good and harm. All phenomena arise because of our thoughts, and as our thoughts cease, all phenomena cease to exist. We may not be able to control how the world changes outside us, but as long as we have self-assurance we are our own masters. Even if heaven and earth are about to fall apart, we will not be affected if our minds are calm and settled.

Self-Respect

The worst thing that can happen to a person is to lose his or her self-respect. It is the best capital we have in life. Self-respect is not arrogance, self-importance, bravado, or over-confidence. It is not surrendering in the face of oppression or authority. It is upholding our stance and principles, and maintaining our character and morality.

Self-respect is not looking down on everything and everyone or being arrogant because of our talents. It is diligently adhering to our sense of propriety. In Chinese history, there are many examples of much sought after ministers with principles and loyalty, who refused to compromise their self-respect for a position under a different ruler. They were "loyal subjects not serving two masters and pious women not marrying two husbands."

During China's Warring States Period, Yanzi was sent as the ambassador to the Kingdom of Chu. The king of Chu asked him to enter through a small side door because Yanzi was a short man. Yanzi refused to suffer such indignity and said, "Only ambassadors to a dog country should take the dog's door. Since I am the ambassador to Chu, it is inappropriate for me to enter from that door." The Chu king was left with no choice but to open the main gate for him.

The wife of Zengzi insisted on being "straight and inadequate rather than biased and sufficient." Famed poet Tao Yuanming refused to compromise his dignity for food. General Wen Tianxiang would rather die than surrender to the enemy, inspiring his adversary, Yuan Emperor Xi, to honor him with an elaborate burial. Chan Master Daokai refused to tell a lie for a pardon and earned the respect of others. They were all examples of not being "subdued by force, moved by poverty, or compromised by wealth."

The warriors of old who engaged in duels were often noble enough to allow their injured opponents to receive treatment for their wounds. In not taking advantage of others when they were down, they preserved their own self-respect. Other people who lost a battle believed that "a knight can be killed but not humiliated," and they preferred to die instead of suffer humiliation. They were also protecting their self-respect.

We humans must live with self-respect. Nowadays, many advocate euthanasia in order to die with dignity. After the September 11 attacks, the media did not take photos of the victims. Their actions were both respectful and ethical.

In nature, some animals also exhibit self-respect. One way they express it is by not feeding on rotting carcasses. In terms of plants, "Without enduring the severe winter cold, how can the plum blossoms bloom so fragrantly?" "While water lilies fade without shelter from the rain, the branches of chrysanthemums proudly withstand the frost." "Leaves of pines and cypresses are the last to fall." They all symbolize great courage and dignity.

Fang Dongmei is a contemporary philosopher and an expert on Huayan teachings. He once went swimming and almost drowned. As he struggled and cried loudly for help, he suddenly thought to himself, "How disgraceful it is for a philosopher like me to act so frightened and frantic in the face of death! What use are the theories that I teach everyday?" After changing his thinking to preserve his self-respect and letting go of his body and mind, he finally relaxed. He ended up saving his own life because he stopped struggling and floated back up to the surface of the water.

Self-respect is being neither haughty nor servile. It means not being moved by gains nor threatened by power. Self-respect is having a sense of shame and humility, because a person without shame is like a tree without bark. Therefore, self-respect is truly essential.

Having Meaningful Interests

Life is not all about putting food on the table and clothes on our backs. It is also about service, contribution, art, and leisure. It is especially about developing many interests in our lives. A life of meaningful interests can make even eating and putting on clothes feel different.

Life is not all about money and desires either. There are people who are wealthy but unhappy. They live in mansions surrounded by butlers and maids and have limousines with chauffeurs to drive them around. While they may not have to worry about their livelihoods, they are miserable because they lack interests in their lives.

So how do we develop meaningful interests? We can, for example, take up reading, hiking, tea drinking, chess, gardening, or discussing the Dharma or Chan with friends. Former President Clinton either spends his vacation with his family, travels, or goes to church for Sunday services. The late Princess Diana stayed home raising her two sons or did charity work when she was not busy with her royal duties or social life.

In the past, Chinese emperors would occasionally tour their empires disguised as commoners. Their aim was to experience a lifestyle that offered different interests than those of the imperial palace. Famous literati would often congregate to recite poetry and share calligraphy, delighting in the immeasurable pleasures of literature and the arts.

These luminaries of the past were not as keen on rich food or fancy drinks as people today are. They were content with a plain bowl of rice and a cup of tea. They lived a simple lifestyle without too many worldly desires. They might sit in a pavilion, sip a little wine, and speak of the mulberries and flax they were growing. They would sometimes let out a roar to relax or stroll by a clear stream and compose a poem. Although their lifestyle was simple, it was certainly not without pleasurable interests.

Some people love to draw because it brings color to their lives, and others prefer to sing because it adds melody to their daily routine.

Writing, practicing calligraphy, or going to a church or temple can bring interest to a person's life. When Ernest Hemingway sat by the sea, watching sea gulls fly and enjoying the sounds of the waves, he found life very interesting. When Albert Schweitzer went to Africa to help the poor and the sick, he was spiritually enriched in spite of the harsh living conditions because he found meaning and interest in life.

Some people are addicted to a life of sex, alcohol, and money. Every night, they visit clubs and go to parties in pursuit of fleeting pleasures, but when they wake up in the morning, boredom and misery fill their hours. They have yet to discover what they are truly looking for. Some people surf the Internet hoping to bring some excitement to their lives, but once they become tied to their computers, not only do they fail to find any other interests, they also become burdened with the urge to be online all the time.

In today's society, people invariably look to the outside for glitter and amusement. They have, thus, lost themselves in their search because their lives are devoid of any real, meaningful interests. So how do we cultivate interests in life? This appears to be a crucial lesson for people of the 21st century to learn.

Having Tastes in Life

As humans live, so do animals and insects. However, not only do our tastes in life differ from theirs, but even among people, there is extreme variability. There are people who indulge in eating, drinking, and having fun. Some people pursue fame and fortune. Others enjoy being around people and gossip, and there are those who spend time idly, not doing anything in particular. Such tastes in life are not what we should pursue.

Life should be filled with the arts, serving the community, recreation, and physical exercise. Many people find gardening, reading, writing, and teaching enjoyable. Throughout Chinese history, there were scholars who took in men of talent and virtue and established schools, because learning was their taste in life. During the Song Dynasty, Lin Bu lived the life of a recluse, raising cranes and planting plum trees as hobbies. The Tang Dynasty's Chan Master Damei Fachang lived off nature in the woods, setting high standards for a hermit's life.

A French writer once wrote, "It would be best for a person to work in Luxemburg (highest wages), drive a German car (best engineered), buy a house in England (best equipped), live in Portugal (best climate), and retire in France (longest life-span)." That would be living the ideal life!

In reality, life is not just about pleasure and riches. We should not be enslaved by money, but rather, we should enhance our interests and tastes in life. When we have time, we should meditate for half an hour to experience the taste of living in tranquility. We can play a game of chess or bridge with friends, enjoy a cup of tea at a teahouse, visit an art museum, or join a book club. We can take part in a Dharma function, write a poem, sing a song, recite a prayer, listen to the bell of a temple, make a pilgrimage, work as a volunteer cleaning streets or visiting the sick, and be a part of those sharing their love and care with the community. These pastimes can all enrich our tastes in life.

We can also have fun with friends in the great outdoors and immerse ourselves in nature. We can share the joy of flowers and relish in the delights of mountains and rivers together. We can extend to others means of convenience, such as building bridges, offering the coolness of shady trees, or relieving their thirst like sweet spring water. Therefore, assuring our value to others should be the main taste we pursue in life.

Interests and Enthusiasm

Regardless of what we choose to do in life, we must do it with interest and enthusiasm in order for anything to last. We must not let boredom and apathy interfere with our work and activities, such as reading, drawing, singing, or traveling. As long as we are enthusiastic in pursuing our interests, there will be hope and meaning in life.

However, our pursuits can be either good or bad depending on what kind of interests we nurture. For example, if we are interested in language, we will be engaged in learning new words. If we are interested in writing, we will be happy writing in journals or reading a good book. On the other hand, if we are interested in gambling or wasting our lives, we will develop nothing but bad habits that are repulsive and unacceptable to society.

We are not born with an innate ability to have fun or be interesting. It is not in our genes to like or dislike certain things. Any wholesome interest must be cultivated with the right perspective. For example, it is wholesome for us to nurture an interest in reading and helping others. If we immerse ourselves in such interests, we will have no trouble getting through our days feeling as if we were in heaven. However, there are people who have no interests in anything they do either at work or in leisure. What is the meaning of life when every living moment is spent in boredom and apathy?

We all come into this world with the potential for happiness. There is the beauty of nature, such as that of mountains and rivers, for us to enjoy. We can admire trees, flowers, and stars in the sky. We have our families and loved ones to give us tender loving care, society to fulfill our every need, and people with whom we can have many meaningful relationships. If we want to repay our debt of gratitude and show our appreciation for all these positive conditions, we should develop our interests in good and wholesome ways.

Any interest we develop should be in good taste because they will be judged by others in the community. We will not be accepted socially if our interests infringe on other people's lives. It is like gaining the kind of freedom that violates others' rights to life and happiness. Since nurturing interests is never a license to do whatever we please, we must abandon our pursuits when they appear to be intrusive or offensive to others.

In making good friends who share our interests, we can enjoy ourselves more than ever. In successfully completing a task that brings us much praise, we develop confidence and expand our interests. We can even make eating and walking fun when we approach them with enthusiasm. Overall, if we can cultivate our interests to embody the essence of goodness, we will gain an inexhaustible treasure.

For example, when we attend a lecture, we should be attentive. When we listen to a story, we should focus our attention. When we see the world, we should find it very interesting and enjoyable. If we can live our lives accordingly, we will be very happy, with smiles on our faces everyday and even in our dreams. However, if we allow boredom to set in and take hold of our lives, we will be very unhappy and unpleasant. It is such a shame for anyone to go through life without interests and enthusiasm.

New Branches on an Old Trunk

Many years ago in Taiwan the old guards and young Turks of the Nationalist Party were fighting for power, and Madam Chiang in New York mediated between the two groups. She spoke on the importance of preserving an old tree trunk, and more importantly, the importance of growing new branches.

When both the old trunk and new branches work together, life can thrive. This concept is applicable to many different matters. The lifespan of trees is even longer than that of people. However, with time trees also age, and if an aging tree can no longer grow new branches, its life will end soon. On the other hand, if new twigs emerge, the tree's life can be sustained and its future is limitless.

It is the same for humans. Just as the waves overlap one another in the Yangzi River, new people will replace old ones. So the older generation needs to hand the baton to the next one because the latter is the key to sustaining life. Even as wild animals, such as lions and tigers, look after their young with utmost care to assure continuity, life also carries on endlessly in this manner.

China with its five thousand years of history has relied on passing down its traditions and culture from ancestors to descendants one generation at a time. As a result, Chinese people and culture are branching out to all parts of the world today. However, for other ancient cultures like Babylon, because the old trunk no longer exists, new branches cannot grow, and thus it has faded into history. While the Chinese enjoy ancient traditions, new technology continually enriches the culture so that new branches continue to develop from the old trunk.

An old trunk needs new branches to sustain life, just as the branches need the trunk as a foundation. Only by being able to withstand the test of time for a thousand years or more can a tree be revered as having spirit. In China, there are hundreds of old stores and one-thousand-year-old plus temples such as Tiantong Temple and Asoka Temple. They still exist because the old trunk and new branches have thrived on one another, sustaining themselves through many generations and still exuding the light of life.

In Taiwan today, most of the founders of Taiwan's largest business enterprises are aging. They have become old trunks. Fortunately, their children have received a modern education and are able to accept the baton by becoming new branches. We hope these old trunks will continue to cultivate new branches and the latter honor and respect the former. When the old and new are able to complement one another, Taiwan's businesses and industries will be able to accomplish even more in the future.

A forest needs old trunks and new branches in order to remain healthy. Similarly, a family needs both in order to thrive. A country requires as many old trunks as new branches. Without enough new branches, which are the life force of the tree, old trunks cannot be strengthened. However, when there are too many new branches, old trunks will not be taken seriously, and social crises might ensue. Therefore, it is the good fortune of any country when there is a balance of old trunks and new branches working together.

Passing the Baton

In public service, retirement is mandatory. When it is time for one to retire at a certain age, the baton should be passed on to the next generation. In the world of sports, athletes are often limited by the extent of their physical strength. Once they reach a certain age, they need to pass the baton so that younger athletes are able to take over. The vitality and morale of the entire team can then be sustained.

Chinese in general are not keen about the idea of passing on the baton. Emperors of ancient dynasties always died leaving their heirs to fight over the throne. Nowadays, some of those in charge of organizations and family patriarchs not only refuse to pass the baton, but rather, as one writer commented, choose to "hit you on the head with it!"

Because the Chinese are uncomfortable with the idea of passing the baton, by the time some of them finally do so in old age, the ones taking over are themselves way past their prime. Some young and vigorous talents are eager and able to show the world what they can do, but they are unable to do so due to nepotism at the top. Thus, they become loyal and docile. After seeing that they have been submissive and obedient long enough, their superiors may eventually decide to reward them with more responsibility. But, unfortunately, because of their habitual conformity, they may no longer be able to make the most of the opportunity.

In a 400-meter relay, even though a runner can carry on after finishing his/her own leg of the race, he/she still has to pass the baton to avoid violating the rules. He/she must let the next runner continue on in order to win the race.

There is really no one-man show in this world. Every accomplishment is the result of teamwork and many causes and conditions. There are also many endeavors that cannot be completed in just one lifetime, but require the efforts of many generations. Enterprises that are passed from one generation to the next are able to last over time. Otherwise, they are only good for the short term. In being able to pass on the baton without interruption, we can sustain the relay and be assured of endless hope.

In Buddhism, there is a tradition of handing down the light. In every school of Buddhism, the patriarchy is passed on from one generation to the next. Likewise, the American presidency is also passed on from the first to the second, and so on, with each president being allowed to be re-elected only once as limited by the Constitution. In ancient China, the ideal was for the emperor to pass on his throne to the most capable person other than his son. This was intended to benefit society and ensure social justice. Likewise, today some open-minded entrepreneurs also pass on leadership positions to their most able executives instead of to family members.

In traditional Buddhist monasteries, the position of the abbot was passed on to the wise and able. In doing so they were able to receive the capable and cultivated from all directions. In today's society, we should selflessly pass the baton to capable young people in a timely manner in order to ensure progress and prosperity. When we do this, we pass on our experience for the next generation to use to improve themselves. At the same time, we enhance the harmony and progress of society.

Getting On and Off Stage

In the course of life, no matter what role we play, we usually have to get on and off the stage a few times. In an opera, for example, the actors get on and off stage between scenes all the time. Several decades of life can indeed pass by quickly while we are getting on and off the stage of life.

It is only natural for us to get on and off stage, to rise and fall in life. Newlyweds start a new phase of life as they proceed to another stage after marriage. Teachers have to prepare before they step up to the podium. Then once the lesson is over, they must step down. Musicians perform on stage and must leave after they are finished. Politicians step onto the stage of politics after they are elected or appointed and should be ready to get off when the time comes. Therefore, in order to feel carefree, we must be able to rise and fall as necessary.

A high school principal in Taiwan left his post and started as a student again. He continued in his studies and earned a doctorate degree as a result. China's Deng Xiaoping rose and fell three times in his political career and ended up being the supreme leader of the country.

Getting on stage, however, is not always a good thing. On some days, we earn applause from all around, and on others, we are heckled endlessly. In general, when we get on stage, if we want to be accepted by the entire audience, we should bring more than laughter to them. We need to keep them satisfied so that our time on stage is worthwhile. After all, if we fail to perform well, it will not be easy for us to get up there again.

Therefore, we should get on stage when we are needed and get off as appropriate. We should not just barely make it up to the stage, since we need to be able to perform right away. Instead, we need to rehearse and practice ahead of time, before our performance. Some people go through all sorts of difficulties to get on stage, but once on, they do not always get the applause they are looking for. On the other hand, those who remain offstage and behind the scenes can still quietly contribute toward society and their country.

Some people stay on stage for only a short while, but they are still able to make history for themselves and humanity. There are other people who neglect their duties while holding on to a position. They achieve little or nothing, their decades on the stage just slipping by.

In the past, some people took great risks fighting for the throne. However, after Qing Emperor Shun Zhi ascended the throne, for example, he began to admire the easy life of his subjects offstage. Nowadays, after every election, the winners rejoice and losers are dejected. In reality, we should practice the Chinese philosophy of "No arrogance in winning; not giving up in losing," and "No joy in gain; no sadness in loss." Since we all have to get on and off stage anyway, we should take all our rises and falls, gains and losses in stride. In doing so, we will be truly qualified to get on and off over time.

Life itself is a stage. We get on it when we are born, and when our worldly conditions are over, we have to get off. According to a Chinese verse, "Why bother fighting over who is stronger and the winner? All these troubles are nothing but a play. Once the drums and gongs cease, we don't even know where home is." Life's firecrackers, applause, and the sound of drums and gongs are only accompaniments for us to get on and off stage. They remind us how impermanent everything is. If these sounds all cease at once, where is our stage in life?

Therefore, people should not be too anxious about getting on and off stage. There is no need to fire cannons saluting our ascension, and there is no reason to be sorrowful when we descend. It is best for us to pay little attention to the process. By being able to establish merit, morals, and good teachings for society, even if our voices, faces, or laughter do not appear on stage, our contributions will always remain in the world to benefit others. That alone would be a major achievement.

One's Standing in Life

People often fight over their position or standing, i.e., they want to be first, second, etc. Even when they already hold high positions, they still bicker over where they stand. Therefore, many people spend their whole lives fighting over their standing.

Politicians are especially calculating when it comes to positions. During public assemblies and meetings, they often argue over how many votes their parties have and where they stand. In school, students from primary school to college and even graduate school are graded on exams to determine their standing.

It is good for a person to pursue the highest position. However, as the saying goes, "The acorn that stands out rots first." People easily get jealous of those in positions that are higher than theirs. So some people now advocate "the philosophy of being second."

There are many lists of "standings" in the world. For instance, there are lists of "Who's Who," the 100 wealthiest people in the world, the top 100 highest paid CEOs, the top 100 scholars, the top 100 universities, etc. Even in religion, there is the standing of different religious leaders. The Australian Immigration Secretary, Phillip Roddick, once asked, "Who is the first amongst the world's religious leaders?" To that I replied, "Whoever you like the most is the first."

Even our fingers and thumbs seem to compete for first place. When the thumb goes up, it signifies the best. The index finger points here and there, directing others like the top boss. The middle finger is the longest. The ring finger often wears gold and silver jewelry and, therefore, stands out full of sparkle and glamour. When they finish making their claims, the little finger says, "When we join palms to show respect to others or when we pray before a saint, I am closest to him/her; thus, I am first!"

Good parents should treat their children equally because their children are like the palm and the back of the same hand. There should not be any distinction as to who is favored more. However, parents who do not know how to teach their children will often say, "The youngest is the best, the oldest is not bad, and only the one in the middle always makes me angry." When parents assign their children different status in the family, their children will also honor and respect them differently.

The following joke is about an award ceremony. When the music played, only the second runner-up was on the stage. The first prize recipient got too excited and fainted, and therefore was unable to receive the award. The first runner-up was upset about losing and refused to accept the prize. The third runner-up was too embarrassed to receive the prize since she was not one of the top three. The fourth runner-up said, "Since the first four did not pick up their prizes, it doesn't look good for me to go up either."

In reality, being first is of course good, but coming in second or third is not bad either. By being able to accept any position, our lives will be easy and happy no matter what position we achieve. Therefore, we should not become too attached to our standing in life!

Places and Positions

When we were little, we played "musical chairs," a game whose objective may have had a lasting impact on us as adults. Conflicts, comparisons, and arguments often arise from the need to compete for the most desirable position. Sometimes, we even forego our own stability and choose a future that is uncertain or volatile so that we can jockey for the best position available.

The game of "musical chairs" is a frequent occurrence in government whenever a new administration takes office. As important posts become available, more and more people vie for the most powerful jobs. Similarly, when a new manager is brought in to make some changes, panic and uncertainty drive the existing personnel to quickly reposition themselves. Whether it is in an office or a classroom, it is natural for people to seek the best seat. We even vie for the best burial site for the deceased according to the custom of *feng shui*.

If a seat is comfortable, it becomes everyone's target. While it is common for people to seek what is comfortable and rewarding, they must realize that they have to shoulder the responsibilities that come with those positions and apply their effort, thoughtfulness, and wisdom. If they lack any one of these requirements, they feel ill at ease in their position. Even celestial beings are not immune from the "five signs of decay" after they have exhausted their acquired merits. In addition to flowers withering on their heads and sweat coming from their armpits, just like others they can become uneasy and anxious about their positions.

Nowadays, it is customary for people to change jobs on a regular basis or seek new affiliations because they are disillusioned with their old ones. It is this dissatisfaction that has caused soldiers to dodge their duties or monastics to return to secular life. Others may be at a loss when a position is taken away from them, and feel as if life is no longer worth living anymore. However, there are people who are comfortable with whatever position they are given or with no position at all, because they are at ease under any circumstance.

The following is a question for all to ponder: "In a human pyramid, which position is most desirable?" If one is on top, one can fall and get seriously injured. If one is at the bottom, one can be painfully crushed, and if one is in the middle, one might not have the excitement of being at the top or on the bottom. Therefore, it is difficult to be in any position without having some complaints. It is important to keep in mind, then, that from an objective standpoint, whenever praise is given for a certain accomplishment, it is usually bestowed on the whole pyramid and not on a specific position in it.

It takes the right causes and conditions at the right time for a person to be in a certain position. It is said that "Places of good fortune are taken by people of great merit." While it is difficult for us to find the right position, it is much easier for the right position to find us. For instance, in today's society, a job is sometimes hard to find. But as long as we are truly qualified, nobody will question our ability and deny us a position we deserve.

Every star in the universe has its own bearing; every tree in the forest has its own roots. As long as we are willing, we will have a place in this world in whatever field we select. The question is, "Will we be satisfied with what we have?"

Teamwork and Division of Labor

No matter what we do in this world, if we want to be successful and effective, we must cooperate with others. For example, our body parts must work together for our bodies to function properly. In order for us to walk, our eyes need to see, our ears need to hear, and our arms and legs need to move. Only through cooperation can we succeed in life. Only with teamwork can we be accomplished in our work.

The human hand has five fingers, and no one finger can lift a thing without the aid of the other four fingers. When all five fingers function together, the hand as a whole will be nimble and forceful. If we want to start a campfire, we need a pile of wood instead of just a single twig. In this world, nothing can be accomplished without the proper causes and conditions coming together and collective effort. Therefore, we should not be jealous or dismissive of others, because teamwork is necessary to achieve a common goal. By working together, we not only give others a break, but also do ourselves a favor.

Three people once lived in a house. One was blind, another mute, and the third crippled. One day the house caught on fire. Out of desperation, the blind man asked the mute man to carry the crippled man on his back, so the latter could bark out directions to the door, while he himself could follow them. Following the directions of the crippled man, all three were able to escape the fire unharmed. The moral of the story is that by working together, nothing is impossible. Teamwork and cooperation always guarantee success.

All things under the sun materialize and thrive only when the proper causes and conditions come together. A house is a house only when all the building materials are present. When minerals are separated into small molecules and processed to form a new compound, we end up with synthetically-derived materials such as fuel, rubber, or fiber. Musical performances are beautiful and harmonious only when the orchestra and the choir work as one. In business, there are partnerships and investment groups. In world politics, there are the United Nations and the NATO forces. Drops of water come together to form rivers and oceans; and grains of sand form hills and mountains. Greatness can only result from togetherness.

Although teamwork is important, division of labor cannot be overlooked, because it assures individual duty and responsibility. A manager must know how to delegate authority to his subordinates, because in doing so, he can allocate work more effectively. On the other hand, workers must work together and cooperate with one another to bring into full play the spirit of teamwork. Cooperation and division of labor, therefore, go hand in hand in producing the best results. They allow managers and workers to arrive at a tacit mutual understanding as members of the same team, working together and in sync to complete tasks. Ultimately, teamwork and division of labor are the best ways to overcome the deficiencies of individuals.

In the human body, the eyes, ears, nose, and tongue all have their own functions. This is the body's division of labor. The hand has five fingers, but when closed, the fingers form a fist. This is the cooperation of the hand and fingers. However, for the whole body to be normal and healthy, the six sense-organs, namely the eyes, ears, nose, tongue, body, and mind must work together and complement one another without obstruction; the hand must open and close freely without much effort. In military engagements, forces are often divided into different teams to converge on the enemy from all sides. These examples show that when teamwork is needed, we must put forth all our effort and cooperate with others. When division of labor is called for, we must make suitable assignments. If an organization finds a balance between teamwork and division of labor, it will be sound and well-organized. If it appreciates the need to both delegate authority and encourage cooperation, it will experience fewer personnel problems.

The Mind Painter

The *Flower Adornment Sutra* [*Avatamsaka Sutra*] says: "The mind is like a painter able to portray any object!" A skillful artist can vividly depict landscapes, flowers, or trees on the canvas. The nature of life, whether it is good or bad, graceful or ugly, can also be easily expressed through the hands of artists. Similarly, the mind is an imaginative painter, capable of capturing almost anything.

Although we cannot be certain that there are omnipotent people in this world, we are positive that the mind is indeed all-powerful. We may be confined to a small room, but our minds can travel thousands of miles in an instant. As we walk down the street, our minds can go up to heaven or down to hell in an instant.

Our minds embrace the ten dharma realms, which include four realms of the sages and six of common beings. The four realms of the sages belong to the Buddhas, bodhisattvas, sravakas and pratyeka-buddhas. The six realms of common beings are hell, and that of hungry ghosts, animals, asuras, humans, and devas.

As the mind wanders between the ten realms, it can take up the roles of different beings within these realms. Sometimes we have the minds of Buddhas and bodhisattvas, and other times we are like animals or hungry ghosts. *The Lotus Sutra* [*Saddharmapudarika Sutra*] elaborates that each realm can also generate its own ten dharma realms, and in turn, each of these dharma realms embodies ten essential characteristics. This is the meaning of "A hundred realms with a thousand characteristics" as depicted in the *Lotus Sutra*. It is a profound philosophy that conveys the infinite capabilities of the mind as a painter.

The mind is like an artist, sometimes painting the world's most beautiful scenery, and at other times, the darkest alleys on the run-down side of town. It is like a sculptor, capable of crafting adorable statues of angels and goddesses, but also scary figures of demons and funny caricatures of clowns. Likewise, the mind is a musician that can play delightful and melodious music or sing a moving or sad song. It is a builder capable of building luxurious mansions, as well as rustic shacks.

If the mind is so omnipotent that it can build an internal universe at will, then why do we not use its powers for the good of society? Since the mind is a fine artist capable of portraying all phenomena, we should uphold righteousness and sincerity daily in our every thought. We should never allow our minds to slack off or get out of control. We should always have morals in all we do, because our minds can take us up to heaven and, in just a thought, can also bring us down to hell.

We usually wish that others would listen to what we have to say. However, it is even more important for us to listen to our own words. When we manage the mind well, and develop it to match that of the Buddhas' and bodhisattvas', we can open it up and allow it to follow its course freely. In this way, we will be able to realize our truly liberated and carefree self, right here and now!

The Wonder of Contemplation

Descartes once concluded "I think, therefore, I am." Thinking is the driving force behind civilization. People think in order to develop their wisdom. According to Buddhism, "One should listen, contemplate, and cultivate in order to enter into perfect meditative absorption." Confucianism, on the other hand, teaches us to "put learning to practice," and also that "learning without thinking is useless."

The ultimate goal of contemplation is enlightenment. In seeking enlightenment, the Buddha went into deep meditation in order to realize the truths of the universe and life. Therefore, some people say that aside from being a great religious leader, educator and philanthropist, the Buddha was first and foremost a great thinker.

In Chan Buddhism, practitioners become enlightened by asking endless questions. In the pursuit of truth, they never stop thinking. So in reality when they are meditating, they are not just sitting there idly but contemplating deeply.

A literary work takes much thinking and organizing to produce. A painting needs a lot of contemplating and planning before it can come to life on canvass. A sculpture requires not only the power of carving but also the strength of the mind. A skyscraper is not just the result of the joint effort of hundreds of workers, but also the vision of the architect's design.

After all, thought produces reality, and as such, reality is the effect of thought. Based on the Law of Cause and Effect, the great scientists and philosophers of today are all important "causes" as great thinkers. Regrettably, however, modern education does not place much emphasis on the teaching of critical thinking, but instead focuses mostly on applied sciences. The latter can be too rigid while the former is more versatile. When we are able to think and understand more broadly, we can be more resourceful in handling matters and more effective in applying our talents.

The renowned modern Chinese scholar, Hu Shi, once said, "Hypothesize bravely, and prove meticulously." To hypothesize is to think, and to prove is to practice. Over the years, Taiwan has made great strides in the fields of agriculture, industry, business, and science. They are all the result of innovative thinking. Now that people in Taiwan enjoy wealth, material progress and scientific advancement, it is time for them to apply their thinking to improving social harmony, resolving the political unification issue (i.e., reunification with China), and even contemplating how to address the ills resulting from the strife of five-thousand years of history.

We need to train the next generation to learn how to think at a young age. They should start with a question like, "What will I do when I grow up?" As they mature, they should ask themselves, "How can I contribute to society and the country?" Every one of us needs to think, "How can we unite the strengths of people to accomplish the best results?" In large organizations, the question should be, "How can we best share the benefits of the organization with everyone?" Likewise, parents should ask themselves, "How can the home be improved?"

The universe is not necessarily what we know it to be. There are always deeper levels for us to explore and consider. Pure lands and Buddha worlds are established by thinking. So we need to start thinking right now about how we can build a pure land in this world. In other words, the question we need to contemplate is how to establish a peaceful and harmonious society.

On Increasing Positive Thoughts

The human mind never stops working. It produces one thought after another at a pace faster than lightning. In particular, the mind produces two kinds of decisive thoughts–positive and harmful ones. Because of the speed with which we form these decisive thoughts, it is imperative that we always be careful of our mental activities, because positive ones can lead to heaven and harmful ones to hell.

Through awareness of our mental activities, we can rid ourselves of every harmful thought and bring forth every possible positive thought. What is a harmful thought? A harmful thought is a false or misleading thought. It arises when we have perverted views or desires. On the other hand, a positive thought is a pure thought. It surfaces when we have right mindfulness, and sets our minds on the path of enlightenment.

However, since the mind can produce harmful thoughts at any given moment, we must find ways to either prevent them from arising or to be rid of them as soon as they arise. In Buddhism, there is the method of recitation. By repeating the Buddha's name wholeheartedly, our minds will be directed onto the right path, ready to combat any undesirable thought such as ignorance, jealousy, hatred, and greed. But, in ridding ourselves of harmful thoughts, we must also be careful not to fall into the trap of being attached to positive thoughts. In seeking enlightenment, we should not be attached to any thoughts, since having non-thought is the ideal way to practice. Venerable Master Huineng, the Sixth Patriarch of the Chinese Chan School, taught Cao Xi according to this principle: "To have a thought is non-thought and to have non-thought is a thought." In other words, non-thought is true non-attachment, the highest realm of realization. If our minds can be empty of all thoughts, our lives will be truly free. We will be able to accept our circumstances without worry, renounce everything without clinging, follow our minds without hindrance, and go with the flow of conditions without attachment.

Our minds are always full of thoughts and ideas, especially

those that are false and deviant. Everyday, we gossip about other people and haggle over gains and losses as our mind drifts unceasingly between the ten dharma realms. A positive thought will take us to the realms of the Buddhas and the bodhisattvas, while a harmful thought will take us to the realms of animals and evil spirits. As such, our minds and bodies cannot rest peacefully, because we are troubled by endless mental activities.

When we sleep at night, our eyes, ears, nose, tongue, and body will take a rest. However, the mind does not relax or slow down for a single moment because it is occupied by endless thoughts. In order to help us rectify and purify our minds, the Buddha taught the "six contemplations," which instruct us to concentrate on the Buddha, the Dharma, the Sangha, the precepts, generosity, and the heavenly realm. He also encouraged us to contemplate the impurities of the body, the sufferings from the sensations, the impermanence of the mind, and the selflessness of all phenomena, so that we can rid ourselves of wrong views and false thoughts.

A Buddhist sutra states, "The mind is like an enemy that brings misery to the body." Human thoughts are like a thief, a wild horse, or an untamed elephant that needs to be subdued. Therefore, people use all kinds of methods to bring their minds and thoughts under control. Some go to the mountains; others live in seclusion in order to practice.

The human mind is undoubtedly influenced by its perception of the world. Once it is defiled, it loses its true nature. If our minds are full of thoughts as worthless as "cow dung," then that will be how we perceive others. On the other hand, if we use the Buddha mind to look at others, then we will see the Buddha Nature in everyone. So we must constantly look into our minds and examine our thoughts. We must strengthen our resolve to achieve Buddhahood and uphold pure thoughts of goodness, beauty, and truth. Only then will we be able to achieve the greatest cultivation of all–the state of non-attachment and purity.

Self-Confidence

During a contest early in his career, world famous conductor Seiji Ozawa was diligently following the music score, when he suddenly realized some bars of music were not in harmony with the rest. He promptly informed the judges but was rebuffed. After struggling with it for a while longer and trying to decide what to do, he finally blurted out to the panel of music experts, "The score must be wrong!" Upon hearing his words, the panel of judges responded with resounding applause because "self-confidence" was in fact part of the competition.

People need self-confidence because it is an essential element for success. It is very difficult to climb to the top of a high mountain. However, when we have confidence, we can reach the summit. The ocean is vast and not easy to cross, but when we are confident, we can traverse any body of water.

Some people want to walk the entire coastline of Taiwan, bike around the world, sail across the ocean in a yacht, or ride in a hot air balloon from coast to coast in America. Whatever the challenge, success belongs to those people with confidence. If we want to fly high, we have to know what we are doing. When our bodies and minds are clear and focused, we can be our own master and have the confidence to take advantage of more opportunities than others. In the past, people considered women unfit as soldiers or police. Nowadays we see many confident women working as police officers and flying fighter planes, experiencing at least as much success as their male counterparts.

Self-confidence can help us cross the Ganges River empty-handed or lift ourselves out of a dry well. Taking charge of the here and now in Chan Buddhism is also self-confidence. Chan Master Mazu Daoyi told his sister-in-law to listen to the sound of an egg. Because she had no doubts at all, she managed to do so. On the contrary, Chan Master Nanyang Huizhong's disciple squandered the efforts of his master because of his lack of confidence. Chan Master Baiyun Shouduan's recognition of "not being as good as a clown," because his own seriousness betrayed his relative lack of confidence, is another illustration of the same problem.

There is a saying, "If our heart believes we can succeed, then we can overcome any stronghold. If our heart believes that we are going to fail, then even something as easy as turning our hand to break a twig cannot be accomplished." We must have confidence in ourselves and be aware of our strengths and weaknesses before we can chart a course for the future. People without confidence cannot inspire others because when they are not even sure of themselves, naturally they cannot win the trust of others. However, self-confidence is not arrogance, inflating our opinion of ourselves, or being boastful. It is perseverance, a basic requirement for goal setting, and the ability to make a sound assessment of our strengths. People with self-confidence are able to take realistic and steadfast steps toward their goals.

Nine out of ten things in life do not go our way, and we may have a record of failures. However, only we are capable of defeating ourselves in the end. With confidence and strength, everyone can break through the setbacks of failure to gain ultimate success.

Motivating Ourselves

There are many examples of eminent Chinese scholars who have motivated themselves in different ways. For instance, they would self-reflect three times a day, rise to work with the crow of the rooster, and study into the late hours of night. In the course of life, each person should have several ways to motivate him/herself. For example, everyday we can develop the practice of:
1. Saying something joyful to remain happy.
2. Performing kind deeds to benefit others in order to get along well with people.
3. Reading good books to enhance wisdom.
4. Contemplating the images of sages to develop benevolence and beauty.

We should strive to improve ourselves. If we do not motivate ourselves and only rely on others for help, our strength will be very limited. Therefore, we should, "Be aware of the present and know what is wrong in the past," and emulate the virtuous sages. We can vow to "strive against all odds" and "not to rest until the goal is reached." We should read the biographies of those individuals who have written about their hard-won successes. We should do a good turn each day, thus living a life of merit. We need to make broad connections with the benevolent and the learned in order to be influenced positively and to motivate ourselves to improve.

Growing up, we sometimes need the guidance of our parents, the discipline of our teachers, the support of the community, and the encouragement of our friends. However, the most important thing is to rely on ourselves. If we do not motivate ourselves and rely solely on others, it is like relying on supplementary injections, which are external and limited in their effect, instead of relying upon our body's ability to nourish itself with its own healthy blood.

How do we motivate ourselves? Some keep mottoes in clear

view on their desks; Buddhists chant the Samantabhadra Bodhisattva's "*Verse of Caution*" during the evening chanting.

The journey of life is a marathon. While there are people who applaud and cheer us on, they are all just helpful supporters helping to create beneficial conditions. True power lies in our own courage and strength to carry on. There is a saying, "Each person eats and gets filled individually; each person liberates him/herself from living and dying individually." It is, therefore, very important that people learn to motivate and transform themselves.

Expectations and Aspirations

We should all have expectations of ourselves. At a young age, we have expectations of being a good son or daughter, a diligent student, and a popular person. As we grow up, we aspire for a higher education, a decent job, a happy marriage, good children, and a harmonious family. However, only having expectations of what we wish for ourselves is not enough. We should also have aspirations for our country and humanity, and seek to serve the public and establish broad connections with people. We need to project an ethical image of ourselves, be a model for others, and most importantly, we should be good people.

A man should aspire to be a good husband, loving and protecting his wife and children, while a woman should aspire to be a good wife and devoted mother, tenderly caring for her family. Parents expect their children to succeed and bring honor to the family name. Soldiers dedicate themselves to their country on the battlefield, and their superiors expect them to be loyal and diligent. Politicians should aim to perform their job with integrity, while athletes strive to bring glory to their nation. Writers dream of literary achievements that last through the ages, and religious leaders work to alleviate the suffering of sentient beings. All in all, when there are expectations and aspirations, there is hope for progress and success.

If we have no aspirations and simply follow the flow of circumstances everyday with a muddled head, life will lose its meaning. It will feel as if we were living in a dream, uncertain of the direction to take in order to move ahead.

However, some people are unrealistic about their expectations, aiming far beyond their means. For instance, people who are inarticulate may attempt to become lecturers, or those who have poor voices may seek to become singers. Some look for the praise of others, even though they are selfish, lazy, and inept in personal relationships. They are like the crow that flies to the top branches wanting to be transformed into a phoenix.

Therefore, before we hold any expectations of ourselves, we need to truly assess our capabilities and strengths. As an old Chinese saying reminds us, "Whatever skills we are born with are inevitably useful." Our aspirations should be in accord with our talent and abilities. For instance, people who like music but have poor voices can seek to become members of an orchestra. Those who love books but cannot write well can become librarians so that they can enhance their knowledge and serve scholars and other people who enjoy reading. Even the physically challenged can aspire to contribute to society with their capabilities.

Most of all, we should aspire to be someone with compassion, commitment, wisdom, diligence, self-motivation, respect for work, and strength to shoulder responsibility. People with expectations and aspirations will have self-respect, hope for the future, appreciation for what they have, and the strength to strive on. Dear friends, what are your expectations and aspirations?

The Spring of Life

The most precious thing in the world is life; the cruelest is taking life. Life is the accumulation of past good and harmful karma manifested in many forms: creatures flying in the sky, swimming in water, crawling on land, or prowling high in the mountains. They may be amphibious or live in multiple habitats; they may be without legs, two-legged, or multi-legged. They may live as independent, coexistent, or parasitic beings. While most lives have form, some are formless, such as spirits, ghosts, and gods. Life can also be mobile or immobile like plants and flowers.

Life occurs in the continuum of time, space, and even human sentiment. In this world, some life forms feed on others to sustain themselves. For instance, large fish eat smaller ones. However, some beings devote their lives to bringing joy and benefit to others. Virtuous ministers in government, brave generals in battle, and religious leaders serving their communities are examples.

Some people do not hesitate to wield their power, sacrificing the lives of many others in order to fulfill their ambitions. On the other hand, some people would rather give up their fortune and good name for the sake of world peace and the coexistence of all living beings. There are people who use their lives to protect those of others, so their nation can thrive and its citizens enjoy prosperity and joy.

The life of good people will always receive blessings of longevity from others, while that of evildoers will often be cursed to end soon. We should, thus, always cherish the full diversity, meaning, and value of life in order to energize all other lives, so that they too will become rejuvenated and active.

An English philosopher once said, "The brilliance of life is captured in brief sparks, but its reality in ordinariness." In this sense, the green mountains, blue sea, and the blooming and withering flowers within the universe all represent life. In everyday life, people use the beauty of art, the sound of music, the physics of construction, and the inventions of science to express life.

The value of life is love, and its meaning lies in cherishing it. For example, a piece of clothing, a chair, stove, or car should be well cared for so that each can last a few more years. We are extending their lives in doing so.

There is life everywhere in nature. Buddhism teaches, "The three realms of existence are within the mind, and all phenomena are in knowledge." Using the mind and wisdom, we can create a clock or a watch. Without our input, how else can it come into being? In this way, our lives are embodied in our creations. A house built with our design and construction is also filled with our life. We should be aware of the life of flowers and plants. If we praise and nourish them with care, they will flourish. If we treat them harshly, they will wither and fade.

In *Humble Table, Wise Fare* it states, "Spring is not a season, it is a state of mind, and life is not a physical body, but the mind's nature." When we pour life into the stream of the universe, the whole world will jump and dance with us. Then, any season, any age can be the spring of life.

Spreading Joy

"We want to spread joy and happiness all around the world!" What a beautiful and meaningful declaration!

Many people busy themselves building houses for Habitat for Humanity. Their kind deeds provide homes for others, spreading joy in the world. There are those who give generously to the needy. In helping others they, too, are spreading happiness in the world. There are ordinary people who are honest and hardworking at their jobs, and also people who hold high ideals and are passionate in contributing to society. They are all spreading joy around the world. Our community relies on people like them to provide warmth and support. They set an example for all of us. Furthermore, like seeds planted in soil that grow, blossom, and bear fruit, words of praise also can spread joy for many, enhancing the beauty of the world.

The compassionate Avalokitesvara Bodhisattva spread compassion and loving-kindness in the world. Ksitigarbha Bodhisattva went to the midst of hell to free those suffering there. Confucius traveled around the different regions of China to teach and spread the seeds of education. The Buddha traversed the five regions of ancient India to spread the wisdom of the Dharma. Had it not been for these past sages and saints spreading joy and happiness, we would not be able to enjoy the spiritual shelter they have all provided us with to live happy and secure lives today. As the saying goes, "The predecessors plant the trees, and those coming after enjoy the cool shade." Our predecessors have supported us with what we need. What should we be leaving for the generations to come?

We should leave kind words in the world!
We should leave good deeds in the world!
We should leave ethics in the world!
We should leave merit and accomplishments in the world!

Our hope is that those with influence in society can transform culture, morals, kindness, and beauty into seeds of joy and spread them around the world. We also hope the general public can convert their goals, diligence, and skills into seeds of happiness and pass them on to future generations to follow. We hope that those who are passionate about teaching others contribute to education, those who are charitable spread compassion, those who are generous share their advantages, and those who are energetic devote their efforts to helping others.

    The qualities we were born with always serve a purpose in life. We should not harm any sentient beings. We should not damage the environment, or depart from good causes that help protect the earth. Instead, we should spread joy and happiness around the world, which is our prime responsibility toward humanity as world citizens. Even a small flower spreads joy with its fragrance, and a little bird brings happiness with its singing. Condiments add flavor to food and oil lubricates an engine. As supreme living beings, how can we not spread joy in the world?

Interpretations

Wang's friend gave him a pot of peonies, but because some of the petals had fallen they appeared uneven. Someone commented, "Peonies are symbols of prosperity, but since these flowers aren't perfect, your prosperity must be lacking!" Wang was convinced by this reasoning, so he decided to return the plant to his friend. On learning the reason why the plant was returned, his friend laughed and said, "But you can also interpret the uneven peonies as boundless prosperity!"

People can interpret the same matter differently, because it can have many meanings. In Buddhism, we often hear the saying, "The Buddha teaches with one voice, but sentient beings interpret according to their characteristics." In our daily life, we are always interpreting the verbal expressions, behaviors, and looks people give us. For example, whenever a supervisor makes a statement, his/her subordinates will ponder its meaning endlessly. Pondering is interpreting.

Chan koans also require our interpretation through contemplation. There is a famous koan that asks "What is the intention of the patriarch coming to the west?" Its deep meaning requires individual interpretation. If we can interpret well, we may become more enlightened. However, interpretation alone does not lead to enlightenment. In fact, the truly enlightened mind understands or sees into the truth of reality directly without going through the process of speculation, which interpretation always entails. Therefore, to avoid speculating or even misinterpreting the good intentions of others, it is better just to think positively.

Different interpretations bring different results. For instance, Mainland China and Taiwan interpret the concept of "One country, two governments" quite differently. Lottery players may pray to a deity for the winning numbers, but each person may have a different interpretation of the advice he/she receives from the deity. Following a plane crash, we can often determine the cause by deciphering data from the black box. Lab reports allow doctors to diagnose an illness and specify the right treatment. Secret military codes require the interpretive skills of decoding specialists. Financial experts analyze the stock market, and political analysts evaluate the prospects of different parties and their candidates. Scientists interpret the weather, earthquakes, nature, and DNA for us, because such information is not readily understood by the general public. Making economic projections and setting educational goals not only require evaluation and analysis but also interpretation of the results. These inquiries all involve "interpretation" to some extent.

Similarly, in dealing with people, we need to interpret their feelings correctly and use tact to anticipate others' reactions properly. For example, according to a traditional Chinese guideline for new brides, "On the third day of marriage, the new bride enters the kitchen for the first time to make soup. Not knowing the preferences of her mother-in-law, she asks her sister-in-law to have a taste first." When we can read the facial expressions of others and predict how they might react, we are interpreting well.

Before we interpret anything, we should gather sufficient background information so that we do not end up making the wrong conclusions. We need to have the right timing also. Otherwise, in addition to the possibility of not reaching our goals, we may even make a situation worse than it was before. Therefore, those who are wise should hone their interpretative skills through contemplating time, space, worldly matters, human relationships, others' minds, life, death, and themselves.

The Study of Life

Life is a profound study that is difficult to understand. Even though human knowledge has become richer by the day, there are still so many intangible aspects of life that are not known. For example, how expansive is life? How long can life really last? What is the color of life? What is the essence of life? It is indeed difficult for anyone to truly know.

In reality, from the Buddhist perspective of dependent origination, life is continuous, transmitted, evolving, and transformed. For instance, the transmigration between the six realms of existence, the evolving of lower-grade beings and plants into higher ones, and vice versa, are all manifestations of change.

In Buddhism, practitioners often ask, "Where do we come from at birth and where do we go after death?" This is similar to asking, "Which comes first, the chicken or the egg?" With today's scientific advances, there are many more questions regarding life, such as:

1. Should life be cloned?
2. Does cryonics really work?
3. Is it moral to kill and dissect small animals for scientific research?
4. Is it right to use pesticides to kill pests?
5. If we were terminally ill, would it be right to end our own lives? Would that be suicide?
6. Does the family have the right to choose euthanasia for the patient?
7. What is the difference between the DNA of a saint and a hard-core criminal?
8. When an earthworm splits into two and both sides are wiggling, where is its life force?
9. What is the intermediate body?

10. Where do humans go after death?
11. Do humans become ghosts after death?
12. If there are endless life spans, why we are confused and lost from one to the next?
13. What is the life of nirvana?
14. Where do sages and saints such as the Buddha, Confucius, Jesus, and Mohammad live after death? If they are living another life, how tall are they? What do they eat and use? How do they live?

Nowadays, scientists engaged in the study of life do not only research human life. Geologists study changes in the earth's crust, astronomers the universe and solar systems, meteorologists atmospheric changes, biologists animals and plants, microbiologists the division of cells, archeologists the remains of culture and people, and historians the development of humanity.

Though life is profound and difficult to comprehend, it actually amounts to two topics: living and dying. Not only does Buddhism examine the questions of living and dying without bias, it is itself the study of living and dying. For instance, the Avalokitesvara Bodhisattva relieves all suffering and resolves the problems of living. The Amitabha Buddha, by receiving sentient beings to be reborn in his Western Pure Land, is resolving the problems of dying.

The ultimate purpose of Buddhism is liberating all sentient beings from the suffering of life and death. Therefore, in the study of life, we must treat with great seriousness the lessons on how to make the best use of this life in order to free ourselves from the cycle of rebirth.

Metaphors for Life

The stages of birth, aging, and death in human life are often conveyed through metaphors. The following are some of them:
1. *Life is a stage.* Many different roles are played on the stage. There are leading men and women, clowns, the faithful, the treacherous, the kind, and the devious. Together, they all perform the joys, sorrows, unions, and departures in life. But once the curtain comes down, everything is empty.
2. *Life is a journey.* Life is like a hotel. We stay there for several decades. Once we leave, nothing belongs to us anymore.
3. *Life is a dream.* There are sweet dreams and nightmares. We dream we are up in the mountains, or swimming in the ocean. We travel all around the world. But in the end, all is but a dream.
4. *Life is floating leaves.* The floating leaves on the water are as unsettled as our lives. We move from place to place, gathering and scattering with nowhere to abide.

Other metaphors we use include dew, lightning, meteors, and flowers. These all illustrate life's illusiveness, emptiness, and impermanence. They seem to depict life as totally meaningless. However, there are also metaphors that emphasize the positive side of life:
1. *Life is the sun.* In the morning, the sun rises slowly according to people's expectations. In the evening, it sets quietly to the longing of people. This does not mean hope is lost, because the next morning the sun will rise again as always from the east to shine on and warm the earth.
2. *Life is a battlefield.* In any battle, there are winners and losers. Losing is of course depressing. But when there is hope for victory, the ideals of life will be realized.
3. *Life is an ocean.* The billowing waves embrace everything. In the ocean, ships go by without leaving a trace, and fish swim

past without a sound. The ocean gives others convenience. It tolerates everyone. We are free to wander about in any manner we like in the ocean.

4. *Life is flowing water*. By flowing in small streams, water goes across mountains and ridges to moisten all living things. By rushing down in rumbling waterfalls, it paints a breathtaking picture of life.

Positive and optimistic metaphors for life also include sunny days, a poem, a painting, a riddle, and tall mountains. These metaphors all underscore the meaning of life.

Actually, life is really just a chess game! We may not play chess in real life, but we all have to play the chess game of life. With the wrong moves in life we lose the game. But if we make all the right moves, we win. If we want to win in the chess game of life, we need to have high ideals, foresight, broadmindedness, steady steps, and selflessness. Then we will be able to see the game board clearly and play without hindrances.

Enigmas

There are endless questions and problems in the universe that will always represent the enigmas of life. We see some people prosper and sail smoothly all the way, while others struggle with every step they take. Why does the world seem so unfair?

Why do flowers wither and then bloom again year after year? Why does grass become brown in winter and sprout green in the spring? Why do people die and cannot be resurrected? These are all mysteries we face in life.

Why do birds sing? Why do the strong prey on the weak? Why are there so many changes in the weather? Why does the sun rise from the east? Why do thousands of types of animals exist? Why does every human being have to go through birth, sickness, aging, and death? These are mysteries we seek to understand but cannot solve.

Where do people come from when they are born, and where do they go at death? It is a puzzle that can never be fully resolved. All the puzzles in the world regarding "which is first" are problems that scientists cannot explain and that philosophers argue about continually but only succeed in making them harder to understand. Of all the religions, only Buddhism offers a complete theory and explanation about past, present and future, as well as about people's previous, present, and future lives. It addresses all the enigmas of life. For instance, causes, conditions, and effects can explain all the questions posed above. So can karmic deeds, the rise and cessation of conditions, the middle path, and the relationship between emptiness and existence.

Once we are in the midst of a puzzle, it is hard to get out of it. We need to find the answer from within in order to free ourselves. For example, where does birth come from? The answer is from death! Where is death going? The answer is toward birth! Which comes first, the chicken or the egg? It is not a problem of which is first; rather, it is like a clock as it moves from one to twelve and back to one again. So why should we ask which comes first?

We study so that we can have good reasoning. However, we are often deluded by our own intelligence. We study with the goal to think clearly, but we often end up with another mystery to ponder. It is like asking "why" three times about a particular matter and turning it into an enigma when it really is not.

People look to supernatural powers to predict everything in the world and find answers. However, these powers may end up being a greater obstacle and puzzle. Because someone without supernatural power does not know if he/she will die tomorrow or the day after, he/she can still enjoy life. If we have the power to know that death will arrive the next day, can we still be at ease with our present life? If we have the power to see everything in the world, how can we be happy when we foresee so much suffering? If we have the power to hear everything, how can we enjoy human relations when we hear people talking behind our backs or realize our friends are actually deceiving us with their pretensions?

Problems that people fail to solve cannot be explained through research or studies. The enigmas and mysteries of life ultimately can only be resolved through our own enlightenment.

Having Art in Our Lives

What is art? It is the creation of something beautiful. It could be a painting, a sculpture, a song, a building, or even a speech, but no matter what it is, it should have an aesthetic value that others can appreciate. As such, it should be pleasing, compelling, and inspiring.

In his book, *The Importance of Living–the Noble Art of Leaving Things Undone*, Lin Yutang introduced millions of readers to the art of ordinary living. He used humor to show that art resides in every aspect of daily life, whether it is eating or walking, putting on clothes in the morning, or going to bed at night. He reminds us not just to drink tea, but also to appreciate its taste and quality; not just to read a book, but also to try to capture the wisdom in it. Such an approach to life is in itself an art.

We cannot exist without beauty in our lives. Therefore, we must learn to be sensitive to things that are beautiful in order to experience that which is pleasing and enjoyable. In this world, there are people who choose to be vulgar and superficial, because they lack an appreciation of beauty. There are also people who live glamorous lives, because they are attached to superficial appearances. However, if we prefer appearance over substance, we will never know true beauty. We may look at a painting or read a poem but never realize its artistic value.

What we value in art is the idea of "beauty." A flower is especially beautiful when it sways gracefully in the wind. A painting may offer vibrant colors or a serene scene, but it should also have distinct lines and a sense of depth to invite contemplation and to truly be a work of art, a work of beauty.

Art after all is the synthesis of human feelings and wisdom. Artists can express their feelings and ideas through different media, such as movies, plays, music, dance, literature, or painting. No matter what medium they use, the aesthetic value of their work can be perceived with our eyes or ears; however, in order for art to enrich our lives, we must also appreciate it intuitively with our minds and spirit.

Humor can also be a form of art that is important to daily survival. A good joke not only elicits amusement and laughter, but also brings relief to stressful situations. Once, there was a gentleman named Mr. Stone. One day, while riding to a friend's house, his servant accidentally spooked the horse, and Mr. Stone was thrown off the saddle. Instead of blaming the servant, he joked, "Isn't it lucky that I am Stone and not Pottery, otherwise you would be picking me off the ground piece by piece!"

In making light of a bad situation, a kind word or a well-intended joke is an essential part in the art of living. If we want to enjoy a rich, refined lifestyle, we must have art in our lives. We must constantly familiarize ourselves with what is true, good, and beautiful in this world, and not focus all our attention on the pursuit of fame and fortune.

The Painting of Life

What is life like? Life is a painting of mountains and rivers!

In a traditional Chinese painting of mountains and rivers, there are dark and light colors, depth and shallowness, highs and lows, far and near vistas, rising and falling lines, and hints of clarity and shade. Through the different shades of colors in the landscape, we can appreciate the mood of a painting. The mountain ranges and gushing water overlap and are layered with hues of green and blue. Wind and rain may blow hard and rough, whipping the withered twigs and yellowing leaves. These are all portraits of life.

A painting may bloom with vibrantly colored spring blossoms, birds singing amidst the fragrant flowers, or canaries flitting across the long swaying grass as they all come alive on the canvas. Anyone admiring the painting can feel the exuberant spirit of life and its joyfulness and excitement. Life in such paintings is so beautiful!

Yet another painting can be subtle and sparse with only fields of grass and a small cottage with its smoking chimney and a handful of chickens and ducks in the yard. The poverty and simplicity of the scenery convey the hard and challenging life of poor villagers.

There may be steep cliffs and rugged ranges rising high into the clouds in a painting. It is like reaching the zenith in life, always lonely at the top! There may also be small trails on the high cliffs, seemingly leading nowhere like the hardships of life, which offer us few alternatives. Then, the mountains light up on top with colors, matching the shades of the clouds, and the waterfalls have the same hues as the sky. As a light breeze blows across the horizon with wispy clouds and endless green waves surging below, life suddenly looks bright. We feel as if we could charge on and reach for the top.

There may be lush bushes beside a few thatched cottages where old farmers tend to their flower gardens against the backdrop of autumn mountains with reddening leaves, a picture of the quiet and relaxed life of a hermit. Sometimes we see mountains and rivers hugging each other with the sun reflecting off the water, shiny and bright. Such is a painting of wealth and nobility, beaming with boundless majesty.

When the road of life is smooth, it is like a painting with clear bright colors, but when people live in tough times and are faced with setbacks and difficulties, life is portrayed as reaching the ends of the mountains and rivers. However, if they strive on with the will to succeed, they will find a way out of their predicament. So even when the mountains are steep and the roads treacherous, they can still go over the top and make progress along the way.

We live our lives amidst mountains and rivers. Sometimes we feel them welcoming us with open arms, and even heaven and earth are full of love for us. Other times, high mountains block the road and endless rivers seem to lead nowhere. We are left pondering where our future lies.

A painting is the artist's creation. The layout of the painting may be near or far, jagged or smooth, or it may be about mountains or rivers. However we choose to portray our painting of life ultimately depends on our own outlook.

The True Colors of Life

We all have our roles in life. When we play them well, we are showing our true colors. In society, different professionals such as merchants, workers, soldiers, scholars, economists, philosophers, scientists, and statesmen all have their respective true colors. While we should play our roles well, many people go astray. Some young men are violent and belligerent. They consider their behavior heroic, when in reality it is cowardly. Out of vanity, many young girls impulsively shop, equating shopping with the true color of womanhood. However, what they are showing others instead are the colors of superficiality and materialism. When we lose our true colors, we neglect our roles and the essence of being human.

Flowers may be red, white, blue, or yellow, and cloth may be made of silk or cotton. Regardless of the color or material, as long as they stay true and appealing to people, they are exhibiting their true colors. If silk does not look like silk, cotton seems synthetic, red is faded pink, or white appears dirty, then each has less worth.

In Chinese history, many demonstrated the true colors of loyalty rather than treachery. They were martyrs fighting foreign invasion, true heroes of their time. However, there were also court jesters and other characters of all shades and colors. Among famous women figures, the first Chinese Empress Wu Zetian was highly recognized for her statesmanship, while Empress Dowager Cixi of the Qing Dynasty abused her power and position. The mother of Mencius and the mother of Yue Fei, a renowned general of Song Dynasty, were both true representations of compassion. There were many other Chinese women who showed the true colors of young womanhood with their courage, abilities, and principles as well.

Regardless of the time period in which they live, people should make every effort to show their best true colors. Every person is motivated by the need to establish the image he/she wants to portray. He/she may choose high morals, loyalty, a sense of responsibility, or diligence. These are all true colors. Unfortunately, some of us have a tendency to keep going astray and, thus, lose our true colors.

In the chapter entitled "Advice to Brother Yendun" in the *Guwen Guanzhi* (*Anthology of Most Admired Works from Classical Literature*), it is written, "Sculpting an eagle without perfection may make it end up resembling a heron; while drawing a tiger without success may make it turn out like a dog." Similarly, living life in a way that perfectly exhibits our true colors can also be quite a challenge.

Human Nature

Everything in this world has its own nature. For example, solidity is the nature of the earth; dampness that of water; heat that of fire; and movement that of the wind. Animals in turn have beastliness as their nature, while demons have evil as theirs. Benevolent and malevolent people each have a distinctive nature of their own as well.

Generally speaking, humans are such by virtue of being endowed with "humanness;" Buddhas are such by virtue of their fully realized Buddha Nature. Human nature is the quality that is shared by all human beings. It encompasses characteristics such as loving-kindness, compassion, universal love, humility, shame, and sociability. Over the ages, countless mothers have embodied the compassion of human nature, sacrificing themselves unconditionally to keep their children out of harm's way. In times of war, soldiers have relied on courage and loyalty, selflessly defending their country and compatriots from enemies.

When the Titanic sank to the bottom of the Atlantic Ocean, fear and panic filled the nighttime air as people struggled to find their way onto the lifeboats. Amidst the sea of chaos and death, an elderly couple calmly put their arms around each other and waited peacefully for their end to come while yielding the way to others. They chose to embrace the ultimate beauty of human nature. When Oscar Schindler compiled a list of Jewish workers whom he could save from the horrifying fate of the Nazi concentration camps, he gave them a ray of hope in the face of human ugliness. There are many other examples in history of how ordinary citizens can become extraordinary in their acts of heroism and ultimate sacrifice. In doing so, they exhibited both the courage of human nature as well as the compassionate nature of the Buddhas and bodhisattvas.

In today's society, the idea of "humanism" has been widely promoted in all areas of life. Buildings and public facilities are designed to be less cold and more human. Schools and businesses are structured to be user-friendly. Even our prison system has largely attempted to rid itself of inhumane treatment.

It is human nature that has set us apart from animals and other living beings. However, it is not unusual for humans to go against their nature in war, invasion, subjugation, hunting, fishing and the destruction of the environment. During World War II, more than six million Jews lost their lives in Nazi Germany. People of Nanjing, China, were massacred ruthlessly by the Japanese Imperial Army. When Genghis Khan led his troops into Central Asia, he had no qualms about slaughtering his enemies, seizing their horses and cattle, and ravishing their women. These all serve as sad testimony to the human capacity for brutality and ruthlessness.

Humans at times can indeed be more beastly than animals. In a Buddhist sutra, there is a story about a "nine-color deer," which was at once a deer among humanity and a human among deer. It is a perfect illustration of the phrase, "Humans are not without bestiality, and animals are not without humanity." It is not uncommon, for example, for crows to care for their parents when they are old, a dog to lovingly raise four pups or a red-crowned crane to fly thousands of miles to see its master every year. They all display the humanness that can be found in their nature.

Nowadays, terrorism has become a part of our lives. We are constantly under the threat of biological or chemical warfare. Nuclear weapons and ballistic missiles are developed and produced to accelerate the pace of global destruction. Human civilization will eventually be destroyed if human goodness sinks into oblivion and animal bestiality rises to the forefront. Therefore, it is imperative for all of the world's people, especially the media, to report the beauty of human goodness and reduce violence and bloodshed in their coverage.

It is only through our self-awareness in eradicating beastliness, bringing into full play the benevolence of our humanness, and promoting our Buddha Nature that the world and humanity truly can be saved.

A New Spring for the Elderly

As the world's population ages, every country will face serious social problems in the near future. In Taiwan, the number of elderly citizens is growing at a steady rate. The government is busy building homes for the elderly, and even encouraging the general public to accept aging parents into their homes to help solve some of the problems associated with this demographic trend.

However, building homes for the elderly only provides a place for them to live and does not really address their other needs. What the elderly need as they enter the last leg of their journey and move toward the cold winter of life is our care, concern, and understanding, not just proper accommodations.

Some people compare life to the four seasons. Childhood and youth are the spring and summer of life, while old age is compared to autumn and winter. In reality, we should relieve the elderly from the feeling that they are entering a cold season in life. Instead, they should be able to enjoy old age like a warm spring. Children and youth can join the boy and girl scouts and other similar volunteer programs in the community to enrich their lives. Similarly, elderly citizens should have their own social programs so that they may enjoy their second spring.

After retirement, many elderly citizens can easily find work as custodians or in other positions. This shows that many of them do not need to retreat from society when they retire, but are still capable of contributing their time, skills, and experience. However, these may not be exactly new beginnings for the elderly. We also need to energize them with activities so that they can enjoy the fragrance of their new spring in life. Therefore, we suggest the following:

1. Organize senior associations so they can make new friends and be socially active. By increasing their social interactions, they will not feel lonely.
2. Establish senior clubs and centers for them to go to for chess

games, exercise programs, chats, or even mahjong to keep their minds active.
3. Set up day-care centers for them similar to those for young children, as they too need our care and attention. There should be young people in these centers talking with them, telling them stories, and studying with them. These centers should provide the opportunity for seniors to work out so that their limbs stay flexible and strong, and offer programs to alleviate loneliness and to help them resolve problems.
4. Set up senior art centers where they can play musical instruments, sing, paint, practice calligraphy, and write poems and book reports–a place where they are able to sing the song of life again.
5. Arrange tours so that they can travel to the mountains and beaches, and parks and woods the way young people do.
6. Establish manufacturing and processing centers for those who are still capable of working to provide them with physical activity and extra money to supplement their income.

All in all, the elderly should be loved and respected. They have contributed to society and left us their love and morals. We should care for them and repay their contributions so that they can live another spring in life.

Life's Golden Age

To live to a hundred would be wonderful if all the years were golden. However, that is impossible, since life is full of changes, regrets, and illnesses, especially as our bodies age.

For some people, their childhood is a golden age because they enjoyed the love of their parents, a wonderful family life, and all the things they wished for. Growth, the glory days of youth, romance, and freedom characterize the golden age of early adulthood. By middle age, ideals, careers, and the ability to realize goals can be considered a golden age. Eventually, at retirement, playing with grandchildren, gardening, or living out our days in leisure amidst woods and rivers make up the golden age for the elderly.

However, life is often unpredictable and disappointing; therefore, it is impossible to live an entire life of golden years. Some people become orphaned in childhood, suffer abuse, or live in poverty. What golden age is there while struggling in suffering and pain? Growing up, people can experience lost love and unemployment. They have no one to rely on or to understand how they feel. They can only see a dark future and not a golden age. By middle age, they become burdened with family and children, and as their responsibilities grow, they find it hard to fulfill the pursuits of status and wealth. Days become years in their lives of despair and apathy. Where is their golden age? Then, in old age, their faculties may fail them as illness and aging become a part of life. They can truly feel suffering, emptiness, and impermanence, but there may not be anyone to listen to their complaints, not to speak of living a golden age.

Life can be sweet, sour, bitter, and spicy. It is full of gains, losses, and impermanence. In the midst of a golden age, everything changes with time, and nothing can last forever. However, even if times are hard, we should strive to overcome the obstacles and not be defeated by changes. As long as we work hard, however small the success may be, it is still our accomplishment, and we can value it.

What is life's golden age? When we have peace of mind, live every moment with right views, embrace the universe, benefit society, improve our character and perfect our morals, our lives can still be golden even if we have no fame, wealth, power, or position!

Life's Second Spring

In some places, wheat and grains are harvested only once a year. However, thanks to research on improving plant species, rice can now be harvested twice a year. In the past, puberty was recognized as the spring of life, but with all the medical breakthroughs nowadays, a second spring in life is not impossible.

In the first spring of life, we are young and strong, full of ideals, passion, hope, immeasurable confidence, and limitless energy. It is like spring when nature is blooming with life and color. In this spring of life, we bask in its warmth and enjoy all the opportunities the world offers. Therefore, we all naturally cherish our first spring.

However, several decades later, we age and probably retire from work. We become familiar with the flux of human relations, and our spirits may wane like the days of winter. But in reality, if we look closely, every person can find his/her second spring. This spring is not about a change in seasons, but about gaining harmony with people. Age does not have to be about the number of years we live but about our vitality during those years.

Nowadays, many people retire from their jobs in their fifties or sixties. However, they are actually in their golden age and the spring of their vitality. They can achieve much more at that age. Because they are older, they know very well what they want to do and how to accomplish it. Unlike beginners in the apprenticeship of life, they do not have to learn everything from scratch. Instead, they can build on what they already know.

In the second spring of life, we are equipped with a wealth of experience and breadth of knowledge; therefore, we can do many things with much less effort. If we are teaching, we may not need to prepare for class as much, because we can pick any subject and talk about it. In human relations, we are no longer like young people having difficulties relating to others and often offending people as a matter of course. When we are in our fifties and sixties, because of our experience in life, we have learned to speak with courtesy and are able to offer others joy and hope with what we say and do. Is this not an expression of another spring in life?

People in their fifties and sixties are capable of supporting the community as volunteers and also have the time to give advice and guidance on how to conduct functions. With their rich experience they are in the best position to guide the younger generation, especially by example. Theirs is a blooming spring filled with warmth and the focus of the limelight. Why would people not cherish this second spring?

After being a member for twenty or thirty years, members of the Buddha's Light International Association (BLIA) can apply to become Lay Dharma Teachers. They will then be able to travel the world teaching the Dharma, visiting many cities and towns. Or, they can be BLIA volunteers in their own branch temples, conducting functions, leading study groups and teaching Buddhism. They will be filled with joy and their lives will be so much more beautiful and fulfilled. Is this not then their second spring of life?

In the second spring of life, we should not be low-spirited or feel old and tired. We should be like the Always-Diligent Bodhisattva, filled with compassion for all sentient beings. We can progress with untiring steps, spread the seeds of a wonderful spring with both our hands, and celebrate the vibrant growth of all living things in the warm spring breeze. This is something innate in us and achievable, so why should we not just do it? Let us all come together and make the most of life's second spring!

Marathon of Life

Marathon is the name of a place in Greece. In 490 BCE, when the Greek army defeated the Persians at Marathon, Pheidippides ran 26 miles to Athens within a short period of time carrying news of the surprising victory. He ran so fast that he died afterwards from exhaustion. When Greece inaugurated the modern Olympic Games in 1896, they established a marathon race of the same distance to commemorate the heroic feat. Since then, the marathon has become a popular race around the world.

The marathon race is a test of perseverance because it covers a long distance and takes several hours to finish. Therefore, not only does a runner need to be fast, he/she also has to persevere in order to win in the end. But in the marathon of life, does the person who lives the longest win?

There is a Chinese saying, "A person who is sixty years old is only in the first year of a cycle. Real life starts at seventy years, and a person at eighty is still a child. While many celebrate their ninetieth birthdays, centenarians are not so rare." Chan Master Shenxiu lived to 102; Venerable Master Buddhasimha lived to be 117; Ananda, the Buddha's attendant, Chan Master Zhaozhou, and Elder Monk Xuyun each lived to be 120. Venerable Master Bodhiruci, the great translator, lived to 156. Actually, humans all have endless lives. However, there is more to the marathon of life than running the farthest, running the longest time, or having the most perseverance. The greatest test of life is to have achievement.

When marathon runners start the race, we all admire their ambition and courage. Each of them hopes to be the champion. As they race, some pull ahead and others slow down. Some might charge up and overtake others, while some lose wind and eventually lag behind. Naturally, there are always those who carry on, sweating and steaming all the way to the finish line to complete their goal.

Life is also a marathon race. When we are young, we start out high-spirited and vigorous, ready to take on the world. After running a leg of the course and reaching middle age, we find ourselves either ahead of the race or lagging behind. There are those who refuse to be subdued by the marathon and continue to strive on, looking for a breakthrough in the race. And there are those who see others overtaking them in the race and become deflated in their efforts, thinking they are not as good. They lose faith and confidence, or even give up the race halfway. It is truly regrettable.

There are runners with spirit who will still strive on even though they are lagging behind. As we run the marathon of life, we should all have the same spirit and perseverance. Even when we lag behind, we still need to race and persist to the end. Though we may not be the champion or even a runner up, at least we will finish the whole race. That is what is most important in the race of life.

The Transmigration of Life

Christianity teaches, "Believe in God and gain eternal life." However, Buddhism teaches that having faith in the Dharma does not mean we are rid of the problem of living and dying. Rather, we need to transcend this duality. Actually, living and dying are the most natural of matters. Even "The Buddha was born when the conditions were right and passed away when the conditions no longer existed. The Buddha came for the benefit of sentient beings and went away for their sake, too."

Life and death follow each other like a shadow. Those who are born will die and on dying will be born again. Living and dying have no end. So where do we come from before birth and where do we go upon death? Most people do not have a clear understanding of this question.

According to the Buddhist teaching of the Twelve Links of Dependent Origination, sentient beings' "beginningless ignorance" (*avidya*) and their commitment of various "actions" (*samskara*) result in "consciousness" (*vijnana*). As this "storehouse consciousness" (*alaya-vijnana*) develops in a mother's womb and becomes a living being, it is called "name and form" (*namarupa*), the mental and physical components of the living being. Within months, the physical body's sense organs (i.e., the eyes, ears, nose, tongue, body, and mind) mature and are called the "six organs" (*sadayatana*). After the baby is born and comes into contact with the "environment" (*sparsa*), he/she has "feelings" (*vedana*) and positive and negative sensations, which develop into "likes and dislikes" (*trsna*). Further "grasping" (*upadana*) is developed for what is loved and enjoyed. Because of the actions committed by the body, speech, and mind, the "being" (*bhava*) for the next existence is planted. Where there is "birth" (*jati*), there is inevitably "old age and death" (*jaramarana*). Death becomes merely the beginning of another lifespan. Therefore, Buddhism teaches that transmigration of life and birth is without beginning or end.

The cycle of birth and death is a natural law. Chan Master

Zongyan said, "The existence and death of humans are like drops of water. In whatever state, it always goes back to water." Right before Chan Master Daokai passed away, he said, "I am seventy-six-years old, and my conditions in the world are fulfilled. I did not long for the heavens while alive and have no fear of hell at death. I simply place myself beyond the three realms soaring freely with nothing to bind me." In facing living and dying, Chan practitioners might conduct their own funerals prior to death, pass away while sitting or standing, or go in the water singing all the way. Some might even dig their own graves in the mountains and bury themselves. They were so carefree.

The life and death of sentient beings depend on their karma, while the life of the liberated saints and sages is fulfilled upon the strength of their vows. Living and dying is not mastered through anything miraculous. What we really need to transcend is the life and death of our thoughts. Chan Buddhism teaches, "By putting thoughts to death, our Dharma-body can live." In other words, our thoughts rise and cease from moment to moment as indicated in the Mahayana sutras, "The ceasing of the previous thought is death and the arising of the next one is birth." In reality, we face life and death every moment. The birth and death of our thoughts are like a gushing torrent and only "non-thought" can block this flow. But if we are enlightened to the truth of dependent origination and emptiness, we can then be like "A wooden statue viewing flowers and birds, unaffected by any surrounding distractions." We can attain an existence in which life and death are non-dual and non-existent. This is the meaning of the sutra teaching: "There is nowhere to go when the previous thought ceases, leaving the next thought that could arise no place to come from."

Life does not exist only at birth, and neither does it end at death. We are like immigrants at death. We just move to another country. As long as we have the resources for existence, merit, and Dharma wealth, we need not fear living in another land. Therefore, dying is nothing to be feared. Where we go after death is much more important.

Chan Master Daoyuan said, "If there is Buddha amidst living and dying, then there will be no living and dying. If we understand living and dying as the truth of nirvana, then we have no aversion to them and even no desire for nirvana. We can naturally be liberated from life and death." If we can clearly understand this truth and eradicate our ignorance, our enlightenment will liberate us from the delusion of the duality of life and death. Thus, we can settle ourselves beyond the fence of living and dying. Why, then, need we fear death any more?

The End of Life

Although most people see "death" as the end of life, it is actually the beginning of another life like a flower that blooms again in the spring when all the conditions are right. Accordingly, there is no finality to life since death is merely a stage in the endless cycle of birth and rebirth.

When facing death, some people prepare beforehand. They write a will that details any unfinished business or plans for their loved ones in order to pass on to the next life without regrets. Although it is their intention to tie up all loose ends, there are things that are beyond their control.

Generally speaking, a wealthy person can afford a proper burial more than a poor person can. When someone is impoverished, he/she may not even have the means to afford a funeral. It is quite difficult for any low-income family today to shoulder the rising costs of funeral arrangements. Who will pay for the burial plot, the coffin, the funeral service, and other related expenses? There is certainly some truth in the saying: "The poor can afford neither living nor dying."

One of the most bothersome aspects of death is the barrage of opinions offered by friends and family concerning the details of the funeral and the reception thereafter. The bereaved are often left helpless as they are assaulted with a barrage of suggestions, ranging from what the deceased should wear to when the funeral should be held and even to what kind of food should be served at the reception. In the end, the bereaved family members are left wondering, "Since it is our parent who has passed away, why is it everyone's business to make decisions for us?"

To make matters worse, some funeral homes may exploit the opportunity to take advantage of a family's grief. Instead of offering their condolences to make things easier, they try to sell the most expensive arrangements so that they can make a huge profit at the expense of the family, which is helpless and willing to do whatever is asked. Therefore, it is best if we can prepare a will in advance to include all the details of our own funeral. This will prevent additional posthumous unpleasantness.

Nowadays, more and more people have chosen different methods of burial, including cremation, burial-at-sea, and the dissemination of ashes. They wish to spare the earth from unnecessary waste, so they prefer not to take up any extra space even in death. Chinese people have long believed in the practice of properly caring for one's parents when they are alive and rightfully returning them to the ground when they are dead. However, while it is in accordance with the principle of respecting and honoring one's parents, it is not the best way for them to rest in peace. As time goes by, many graves are forgotten and left to stand alone in the wind and rain. We certainly do not want to be so desolate in death.

Buddhist sages of the past were very carefree and gracious in their attitudes toward death and dying. While some died quietly in their seats or beds, others peacefully left this world singing in the water, working in the fields, or reciting the Buddha's name. Some eminent masters even embarked on their journeys without others realizing that they were dead. They all achieved the highest level of freedom in seeing life in death and vice versa.

Death is not something to be afraid of as long as we are carefree and without any attachments. We should leave this world as we entered it, empty-handed and without worldly possessions. What can be more carefree than that!

The Non-Duality of Living and Dying

Our world is progressing rapidly in so many ways, but in terms of the progress in knowledge, it is especially heartening to find that the study of living and dying has become very popular with the general public. Some people are studying it with great interest. Living and dying are realities we all face. In the past, dying was a taboo subject for many people, but nowadays, most of us are able to face it honestly. We no longer avoid talking about it, but rather are intent on lifting the veil covering the topic.

According to custom, we all rejoice on hearing about births and grieve over deaths. We celebrate and congratulate each other when babies are born. Confronting a loved one's death, however, we weep and are deeply saddened. In reality, in being born, we are all destined to die. Humans are born to die, so what is there to rejoice about? When we die, it is like winter passing. Yet spring will come again, so what is there to mourn? Living and dying are the same entity and are non-dualistic. At birth, we have to die, and after death we will be born again. Living and dying, dying and living, it is all a natural cycle. There is nothing to cheer for or grieve over.

When humans die it is like an old house that is torn down to make way for a new one. When the new house is ready for human habitation, is that something to be happy or sad about? An old car is replaced by a new one. When we drive the new car, are we joyful or sad? The aged physical body is like the old house or old car that needs to be replaced. It is a natural process, so we should feel happy not sad.

Humans fear death because living seems tangible, and at death everything seems extinguished. We become saddened when it seems there is nothing left for us. In reality, human life is like a glass of water. When the glass is broken it cannot be restored. The water spilling onto the table or on the floor, however, can be soaked up and put back into another glass. Not a single drop of the water of life is lost. The human body is also like a log. Once one log burns out, the next one begins burning. The logs are different; however, the fire of life carries on.

Learning Buddhism does not mean we are relieved of the problems of living and dying; instead, we should be able to see through them! Living and dying are the most natural phenomena. According to Buddhist teachings, "The Buddha was born when the conditions were right and passed away when the conditions no longer existed. The Buddha came for the benefit of sentient beings and went away for their sake, too."

When the conditions of human life no longer exist, we should just follow the circumstances naturally. In the endless future, we will come again with the right conditions. When we finally accept living and dying as non-dualistic, then why will we need to celebrate birth and mourn death?

Glossary

Amitabha Buddha: The Buddha of the Western Pure Land, also known as the Buddha of Infinite Light. Amitabha Buddha is described as vowing to purify a realm for those who desire to seek rebirth there by earnestly reciting his name. Sometimes referred to as Amita Buddha or Amitayus Buddha (the Buddha of Infinite Life.)

Asura: A sentient being whose arrogant thoughts, words and actions dominated his living and directed the karma or momentum of his intentional life choices to be reborn as an *asura* or malevolent spirit. The *asura* is one of the Eight Divisions of Deities. Although known for his contentious nature, the *asura* is sometimes relied upon as a protector of Buddhism.

Avalokitesvara Bodhisattva: The Bodhisattva of compassion who can manifest in any conceivable form to bring help to those in need. In China, the Avalokitesvara Bodhisattva is usually portrayed in female form, and also referred to as the "Guan Yin" Bodhisattva.

Bodhi: "Awakened" or "enlightened." In the state of *bodhi*, one is awakened to one's own Buddha Nature, thus eliminating all afflictions and delusions. Gaining a *bodhi*-mind can be understood as the attainment of *prajna*-wisdom.

Bodhisattva: An enlightened being. It is a compound word made up of "bodhi" and "sattva." Bodhi means "enlightened" and sattva refers to "sentient beings." Therefore, the term bodhisattva refers to a being that has attained enlightenment through practicing all six paramitas. Bodhisattvas vow to remain in the world, postponing their own full enlightenment in entering nirvana, in order to liberate all beings. The bodhisattva ideal is the main defining feature of Mahayana Buddhism.

Buddha: Literally "The awakened one." Used as a generic term to refer to one who has achieved enlightenment and attained complete liberation from the cycle of existence (see *samsara*). More commonly used to refer to the Sakyamuni Buddha, the historical founder of Buddhism (581-501 B.C.E.). He was born the prince of Kapilavastu as the son of King Suddhodana. At the age of twenty-nine, he left the royal palace and his family to search for the meaning of existence. Six years later, he attained enlightenment under the Bodhi tree. He then spent the next forty-five years expounding his teachings, which include the Four Noble Truths, the Noble Eightfold Path, the Law of Cause and Effect, and the Law of Dependent Origination. At the age of eighty, he entered the state of *parinirvana.*

Buddha Nature: The true nature or inherent potential for achieving Buddhahood that exists in all beings.

Chan: A school of Buddhism that emphasizes enlightenment through deep contemplation, meditation and internal cultivation. Practicing Chan Buddhism does not rely upon intellectual reasoning, analysis of doctrine or academic studies, but instead, relies upon a profound inner concentration that can reveal and illuminate one's true nature. (Synonym: Zen)

Dharma: Literally "law." Usually refers to the teachings of the Buddha. When capitalized, it means: 1) the ultimate truth and 2) the teachings of the Buddha. When the Dharma is applied or practiced in life it is referred to as: 3) righteousness or virtues. When it appears with a lowercase "d" it means: 4) anything that can be thought of, experienced, or named; close in meaning to "phenomena."

Five Contemplations for Eating: Five contemplations practitioners should be mindful of when they take their meals. They include being grateful for the effort in producing and making the food; making sure one's heart and mind is pure and deserving of the offering; guarding oneself against greed in consuming the food; treating the food as medicine to nourish the body; and accepting the food as sustenance on the path of spiritual cultivation.

Five Precepts: Guiding principles in Buddhism that teach proper conduct. They include abstaining from: 1) killing, 2) stealing, 3) sexual misconduct, 4) lying, and 5) ingesting intoxicating substances.

Four Immeasurables: Refers to the four ideal states of mind in Buddhism. 1) the state of boundless loving-kindness in giving others happiness; 2) the state of boundless compassion in liberating others from suffering; 3) the state of boundless joyfulness in keeping others away from suffering; 4) the state of boundless equanimity in treating others equally and without discrimination.

Four Means of Embracing: Four methods used by the bodhisattvas to guide sentient beings on the path of liberation. They are 1) giving, 2) kind words, 3) altruism and 4) sympathy.

Four Noble Truths: A fundamental Buddhist teaching about the nature and existence of suffering: 1) the truth of suffering, 2) the truth of the cause of suffering, 3) the truth of the cessation of suffering, and 4) the path leading to the cessation of suffering.

Guan Yin: Popular Chinese reference to the Avalokitesvara Bodhisattva.

Humanistic Buddhism: The primary teaching of Venerable Master Hsing Yun, which emphasizes putting Buddhism into practice in our daily life, and building a pure land in our living world.

Kalpa: A measuring unit in ancient India, signifying an immense and inconceivable length of time. Buddhism adapted it to refer to the time between the creation and recreation of the worlds.

Karma: Defined as "work, action, or deeds" and is related to the Law of Cause and Effect. All mental, verbal and physical deeds that are governed by *intention*, whether kind or harmful, produce effects. The effects may be experienced instantly, or they may accumulate and not come into fruition for many years or even many lifetimes.

Koans: Literally "public notice" in Chinese that originally referred to a legal precedent. However, this became a term adopted by the Chan tradition to refer to a phrase or question and answer exchange that points to an essential paradox. Contemplation of a koan is aimed at transcending logical or conceptual assumptions in order to intuit the ultimate reality of emptiness.

Ksitigarbha Bodhisattva: The Bodhisattva who is venerated for vowing to save all sentient beings from the torment of hell.

Law of Cause and Condition: A universal truth in Buddhism based on the dependent origination of all phenomena in primary causes and secondary causes (conditions). The seed out of which a plant or a flower grows is a good illustration of a primary cause. The elements of soil, water, sunlight could be considered the necessary conditions for growth.

Law of Cause and Effect: This is the most basic doctrine in Buddhism, which explains the formation of all relations and connections in the world. This law shows that the arising of each and every phenomenon is due to its own causes and conditions, and the actual form, or manifestation, of all phenomena is the effect.

Law of Dependent Origination: The central principle that phenomena do not come into existence independently, but only as a result of causes and conditions. As such, no phenomenon possesses an independent self-nature, but rather is contingent on interdependence.

Mahayana: Literally means "The Great Vehicle," referring to one of the two main traditions of Buddhism, the other being Theravada. Mahayana Buddhism stresses that helping all sentient beings attain enlightenment is more important than just self-liberation.

Nirvana: Literally "extinction," but also can mean "calmed, quieted, tamed, or ceasing." In Buddhism, it refers to the absolute extinction of individual existence, or of all afflictions and desires; it is the state of liberation, beyond birth and death. It is also the final spiritual goal in all branches of Buddhism.

Noble Eightfold Path: Eight right ways leading to the cessation of suffering according to the Four Noble Truths taught by the Buddha. They are: 1) right view; 2) right thought; 3) right speech; 4) right action; 5) right livelihood; 6) right effort; 7) right mindfulness; and 8) right concentration.

Prajna: Literally "consciousness" or "wisdom." As the highest form of wisdom, *prajna* is the wisdom of insight into "emptiness," which is the true nature of all phenomena. The realization of *prajna* also implies the attainment of enlightenment, and is in this sense one of the six *paramitas* or "perfections" of the *bodhisattva* path. Sometimes referred to by the compound term, *prajna-wisdom*.

Pratyeka-buddha: Literally "solitary awakened one." Refers to a sentient being seeking enlightenment through the contemplation of the Law of Cause and Condition not to teach others, but for his own liberation. In the Mahayana tradition, the *pratyeka-buddha* is placed between the *arhats* and the Buddhas who have achieved full enlightenment.

Pure Land: Pure Land practice can be traced back to India and the teachings of the Buddha. It remains the most popular worldwide of all the 84,000 different Buddhist paths to supreme enlightenment. The Pure Land practitioner seeks rebirth in the Pure Land of Amitabha Buddha first through cultivating the *bodhicitta*, or the desire for enlightenment;

second, through the practice of reciting the name of Amitabha Buddha with sincerity and deep devotion cultivating one's life through the three trainings of precepts, concentration, and *prajna*. Together, they enable one to more rapidly purify one's mind and liberate oneself from all delusions. Although one is not free from all wants and fears in the Pure Land, they no longer bind one. The Pure Land can also be found in this world in all its imperfections by the devout practitioner.

Samadhi: The highest state of mind achieved through meditation, chanting, reciting the Buddha's name, or other practices, in which the mind has reached ultimate concentration and is not subject to thoughts and distractions. The highest state of *samadhi* is the "*bodhi*" or enlightened mind.

Samantabhadra Bodhisattva: The Bodhisattva who is venerated as the protector of all who teach the Dharma.

Sangha: Refers specifically to the community of monastics or more generally to the Buddhist community that includes both monastics and laypersons. The *sangha* is considered one of the Triple Gems in Buddhism.

Six Paramitas: Also known as the "six perfections" that bodhisattvas attain in the course of their development. "*Paramita*" in Sanskrit literally means "gone to the other shore," which can also imply reaching transcendental perfection or complete attainment. The six *paramitas* or perfections are: 1) charity; 2) moral discipline; 3) patience; 4) diligence; 5) meditation; and 6) *prajna*.

Sravaka: Literally "hearer." *Sravakas* liberate themselves from the cycle of rebirth by "hearing" the Buddha's teachings and attaining *arhatship*, the ideal in Theravadan Buddhist practice. In contrast to the bodhisattva of the Mahayana tradition, the *sravaka*, upon fulfilling the *arhat* ideal, chooses not to remain in the cycle of rebirth to benefit all sentient beings and instead enters nirvana.

Sunyata: Literally "emptiness" or "void." A central concept in Buddhism, which asserts that everything existing in the world is due to dependent origination and has no permanent self or substance. Its meaning can be applied to two groups: 1) emptiness of living beings, which means that human beings or other living beings have no unchanging, substantial self; or 2) emptiness of *dharmas*, which means that the existence of all phenomena is due to causes and conditions. Unlike nihilism, this concept does not imply nothing exists, rather it stresses that all existence is without independent substance or absolute essence.

Sutra: Literally "threaded together." Refers to the scriptures taught directly by the Buddha, and recorded by his disciples for all to follow in their practice. The direct attribution of the teachings to the Buddha is implied in the opening line of each sutra, "Thus have I heard."

Ten Dharma Realms: The realms of 1) hell, 2) hungry ghosts, 3) animals, 4) asuras, 5) humans, 6) heavens, 7) sravakas, 8) pratyekabuddhas, 9) bodhisattvas and 10) Buddhas.

Ten Wholesome Conducts: Buddhist teachings that instruct practitioners to 1) protect and nurture life, 2) abstain from stealing, 3) abstain from sexual misconduct, 4) speak truthfully, 5) foster good relationships, 6) speak gently and use encouraging words, 7) speak sincerely, 8) practice generosity, 9) practice patience and tolerance, and 10) uphold the right view.

Theravada: Literally "teaching of the elders of the order" in Pali. One of the eighteen schools in the Period of Sectarian Buddhism. Unlike the *bodhisattva* ideal in Mahayana tradition, its emphasis is on the liberation of the individual. In the 3rd century B.C.E., it was transmitted to Sri Lanka from India. Today it is popular in many areas of Southeast Asia.

Three Dharma Seals: Also known as the Three Marks of Existence.

According to the *Connected Discourses of the Buddha* in the Chinese Buddhist Canon, they are: 1) all conditioned dharmas are impermanent; 2) all dharmas are without self; and 3) nirvana is equanimity.

Triple Gems: The Buddha, the Dharma and the Sangha.

Twelve Links of Dependent Origination: The twelve links in the chain of existence or the twelve conditions that keep us in the wheel of rebirth. The twelve conditions are 1) ignorance, 2) activity, conception, and disposition, 3) consciousness, 4) name and form, 5) the six sense organs, i.e., eyes, ears, nose, tongue, body, and mind, 6) contact, 7) sensation or feelings, 8) thirst, desire, and craving, 9) grasping or clinging, 10) being or existing, 11) birth, and 12) old age and death.